SILENT VICTIMS
PART ONE

Three Years Explorin &
Physical Health of Ma   ny

A Family History Series

GARY MILLAR

WRITING ON THE WALL

Writing on the Wall
Toxteth Library
Windsor Street, Liverpool
L8 1XF

Published by Writing on the Wall, 2025

© Gary Millar 2025

The right of Gary Millar to be identified as the Author of the Work has been asserted by him in accordance with the Copyright, Designs and Patents Act 1988.

Design and Layout by Jenny Dalton
Cover Design by Ged Doyle Plastic Design

978-1-916571-18-1

All rights reserved. No part of this publication may be reproduced, stored in a retrieval system, or transmitted, in any form or by any means, electronic, mechanical, photocopying, recording or otherwise, without the prior permission of the publishers.

0151 703 0020
info@writingonthewall.org.uk
www.writingonthewall.org.uk

For My Mum, about whom these case notes and letters were originally written.

'Addiction is not a sin or a crime; it is a condition.'
William Ivor Neil Kessel (1927–1980)
Royal Infirmary of Edinburgh

William Ivor Neil Kessel (1927–1980) was a British psychiatrist and addiction specialist known for his significant contributions to understanding and treating addiction as a medical condition rather than a moral failing. His work emphasised compassion and evidence-based approaches to addiction treatment. Kessel's insights have had a lasting impact on the field of psychiatry and addiction medicine, advocating for a holistic understanding of addiction that considers both biological and social factors. Kessell treated my mother.

'Effective psychiatric care requires both scientific rigour and compassionate understanding.'
Bernard Alexander Edwin Magill (1907–1998)
Bangour Village Hospital, Scotland

Magill was a distinguished psychiatrist, with a career marked by significant contributions to psychiatric medicine, education, and patient care, particularly in Scotland. He also worked with my mother.

QUOTES & COMMENTS

Thank you for sharing your mum's story and the important message attached to it. I am sure so many people can relate, not only the sad circumstances, but medication that causes more harmful side effects. Your mum was a beautiful woman and a true warrior. I don't think there is anyone that can say that they are not battling with something in their lives and it's important to speak out. You are an inspiration in everything you do, Gary Millar, and I am sure your mum is around you feeling proud — **Donna M O'Connor**

Your words are so poignant to me. It has been 35 years since my Mum took her life. Another Mum prescribed a cocktail of drugs and treatments including Valium & electroshock therapy for many years and eventually failed by the system. Thank God that we now live in a world that looks on mental health in a more enlightened way — **Dave Winpenny**

Oh Gary, this brought tears to my eyes and how thoughtful of you to showcase the wonderful mum you had and, by the sounds of it, cherished, no matter what. It is so sad to hear what your poor mum endured and I'm so glad that we now talk more openly about mental ill health and the demons that go with it. I teach about mental health and support people getting their mojo back and I'm so proud of you for doing this. Well done. — **Sue Kelly**

It is a very harrowing story, and amazing that you and Leslie came through as well as you did — **Dr Martin Johnson, former Director of the Thalidomide Trust (2000-2014)**

INTRODUCTION

Prepare to be astonished and shocked. For you are about to learn about my dearly departed mother, Margaret Majorie Millar. Madge to her family and friends. Mum to me and my two brothers. She was a Scot's lass. Fun, yet sad, wise, yet not academic. Her passionate, expressive, and sociable temperament sometimes boiled over from her late eighteenth century Italian heritage. However, you learn that those tasked to help her did not describe her this way. Medical intervention began when she was 17 and increased when she was 24. But considerably ramped up at 27, triggered by the traumatic birth of her third child, Leslie, my youngest brother, in 1962. The drug was said to have killed 80,000 children and later they discovered Leslie was one of only 520 Thalidomide survivors in the UK. However, it wasn't until 1970 that they finally recognised that the Thalidomide drug caused his disabilities.

This eight year post-natal delay meant Mum's uncertainty, guilt and speculation continued to play heavily on her already fragile mind. With often life-changing outcomes.

Continually depressed, she was prescribed sedatives, hypnotics, and anti-depressants. They strangely left her more anxious, paranoid, and, at times, psychotic and suicidal. Furthermore, her doctor prescribed the sedative Thalidomide, touted as a safe wonder-drug, to ease morning sickness, lack of sleep, and, as a result, depression.

Of course, as I grow older, I want to know more. I want to better understand what she went through and as result how I was affected by what I know to have been an extended, but much forgotten, difficult period in my childhood.

So, in March 2024, following my 'Subject Access Request' to Lothian Health Services Archive (LHSA), I received 150 pages describing in sad detail Mum's case file, between July 1962 and August 1965. The documents you will now read include all that remain of her historic health and social care records – although I am surprised to learn that these 3 years of papers are all that appear to exist for her entire life.

I have now transcribed, and include here all those often distressing, sometimes bland and mostly shocking pages. Of course, I have redacted the names of all professionals to protect their identities.

Interestingly, as I was finishing the draft of this book, someone asked me an obvious question. That being 'could I explain why I have written it?' This is surprisingly more difficult for me to answer than I first thought. I really did struggle with my response. I suppose one answer is to help us better understand, record, and reflect on the process and language used to treat and describe patients undergoing psychiatric care in the 1960s. But this answer sounds a little glib and perhaps only scratches the surface. I suppose other reasons, for me personally, is that it helps me better understand my mother, my own formative years and most of all, seeing in raw and difficult detail what she went through because of being prescribed the Thalidomide drug. Through reading her case file, I do indeed better understand her situation and have now been able to tease out and conclude my own long forgotten memories. Plus, the process of me reading and writing her notes has itself been hugely cathartic. It has also been a really useful process in helping me publicly record three of the most difficult and darkest years in her life — and mine!

In terms of my writing style or the language I have used in writing this book, some readers may see it as also being deadpan. That is not my intention. It is factual, with some depth when truly required. But I need to stress that against a background of being on the receiving end of significant trauma between the age of three and eleven, I understandably have limited recall of how I felt back then. I can only assume that emotionally I had shut down to hide what I had gone through. For example, I witnessed and suffered violence at home, often felt significant neglect and experienced relationship trauma as my bond with both parents suffered from repeated disruption. So, my limited use of overly enthusiastic commentary in some of the following pages is because I do not feel angry and often I do not remember the circumstances or the impact. Instead, I am, like you, an outsider, and one that is simply seeing from afar the often-intense situations described. Yes, I was directly and severely affected, but I chose at an early age to invent my imaginary safe space. I achieved this by hyper-focusing on good things, pleasing people, happy memories, and proving that we can improve our lives. Equally, and emotionally, it sadly also helped create a more distant Gary, a young person who struggled with relationships and with early years of education. I was someone who wanted to trust everyone but became disappointed when their actions proved otherwise.

In the meantime, and back to this book, in terms of its structure, on the pages opposite my mother's transcribed notes, I have also included a helpful expansion on that content. In printed form, this means that my comments and reflections will appear on one side of the page and the transcribed original records on the page. However, where the original note requires no explanation, or where my words would not do them justice, I have chosen not to comment. These particular notes are best left to you and your imagination!

I have also not corrected the original spelling, grammar, inclusiveness, language conventions, clarity, or the vocabulary of those notes. For accuracy of what was recorded, I have preserved them in their original written form.

So please read and learn about the underbelly of squalid living, poverty, drug and alcohol addiction, domestic violence and the devastating impact of distressing mental and physical health issues. All significantly made worse by the then unknown and silent impact of the Thalidomide drug.

Join me as we travel back in time to glimpses of the 1930s, 40s and 50s, and to my mother's not so 'Swinging Sixties.'

TIMELINE PRE-1962

This gives you a better understanding of the background to my mother's life prior to the main content of this book.

I did not know until reading her case file about the items marked * to the left side of the years below.

Drambuie launched	1910	Birth of Dad's father
National Insurance Act passes	1911	Birth of Dad's mother
Unionist Party emerges	1912	Birth of Mum's father
Start of First World War	1914	Birth of Mum's mother
End of First World War	1918	
Birth of Scottish National Party	1934	Birth of Mum
First Broons cartoon appears	1936	Disappearance of Mum's mother
Coronation of George VI	1937	Birth of Dad
Start of World War 2	1939	Mum's evacuation during WW2*
Clydebank & Greenock Blitz	1941	Mum attends Stenhouse Primary*
End of World War 2	1945	
BBC broadcasting resumes	1946	Mum attends Saughton Secondary*
Winston Churchill resigns	1955	Death of Mum's grandad
UK's first motorway opens	1958	Marriage of my parents
First hovercraft launched	1959	Birth of first son
First 'Beatles' performance	1960	Birth of second son
First James Bond film Dr. No	1962	Birth of third son

A YEAR OF OPTIMISM

GARY MILLAR

A YEAR OF OPTIMISM

My name is Gary Millar. Apparently, my parents named me after the 'milkman.' Which, of course, might conjure up some interesting and more earthy assumptions. However, I was told instead it had something more to do with milk vouchers being wrongly delivered to Dad's parents — to my wonderful Nana and Grandad Millar. However, I also like the alternative story, that they named me after the 'Yellow Rose of Texas' singer of the same name – who also later sang the TV series Stingray's closing theme 'Aqua Marina.'

Whether 'milkman' or vocalist, I am most definitely the firstborn to Madge and Gordon Millar. I was born a Leo, the first bairn, the wean, a roaring lion cub, in the months before the yet to be swinging 60s.

From reading Mum's case file, I can only assume that with my birth, they were both eager for better years and less trauma. Indeed, Mum must have thought her life could only improve following her previously tough upbringing. Plus, like others, both parents must have dreamed of further recovery from the 1939-45 war as the country moved into an exciting new decade.

Equally, my hometown, Edinburgh, in Scotland,

was changing. It was then balancing its rich historical heritage with the demands of what was being described as an exciting modern future.

So, my birth, against this backdrop, to two doting parents, set the stage for an understandable optimism. In fact, I know the whole family was rather excited, as I was the very first grandson and the first nephew. I know that as a result; my grandparents, aunts, and uncles spoiled me – that is, until the next Millar, a boy, was born, my brother Norman.

Yes, with me, now in their lives, our wider family shared in the excitement of not only a firstborn but also a new beginning, a new decade, and a growing anticipation for something better about being welcomed into a happy New Year, or as we describe in Scotland, a 'Happy Hogmanay.'

Yes, the dismal, threadbare and financially exhausted 50s was about to become something else. So, as the sun set on one year, the sun was about to rise for the next year and a new decade. They expected a more glorious and brighter future. You could say that The Millars were keen for some well-deserved and overdue sunshine.

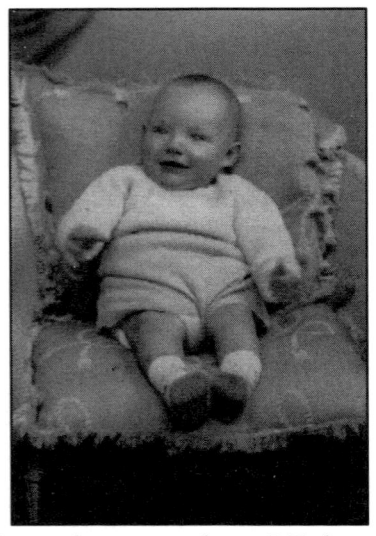

Gary's first photographs – 5 February 1960

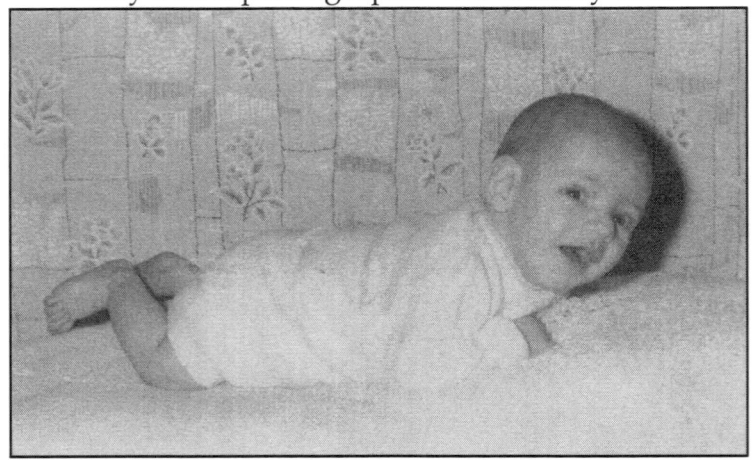

SUNSHINE ON LEITH

GARY MILLAR

SUNSHINE ON LEITH

Sadly, I must report that for the first four years of my life, in this bright new decade, my Mum, my dad, my new second brother Norman and I endured abject poverty and squalid living conditions.

In addition, our lives were about to be affected by a major upset, trauma, hysteria, and Mum's inconsolable tears and alcohol and prescription drug induced screams.

This troubling story takes place in a slum area of Edinburgh called Leith, north of London Road.

Our home, my first, was in the shadow of a football ground, home to 'Hibees' or 'Hibs,' or otherwise sometimes known as 'The Cabbage' – as in the rhyming slang 'Cabbage and Ribs.' Officially known as Hibernian Football Club, they played at Easter Road, only minutes from our small room and kitchen flat.

Every match day, we would clearly hear triumphant stadium roars – but not always from the home side. Whilst they seemed to make a lot of noise, this team in green didn't play too well during my earliest years.

However, one of my positive memories relating to Hibs was more recent when they adopted one of my favourite songs, the terrace anthem 'Sunshine on Leith.' A fine song that today makes me think happy thoughts about Leith being a glorious and sunny place. Except, in my experience, it was then less green, and definitely more grey, sad, and dismal!

Yes, there wasn't too much sunshine in my version of the 'Swinging Sixties.' In fact, the only swinging I remember were the fists and slaps delivered by those we loved.

But this sad story is not about me or the home we lived in. Instead, it focuses on 3 traumatic years in the life of my mother – who, as you will learn, was also known as Madge, Margaret, and Marjorie.

It is a factual story, one based on the physical records held in her case file by the Lothian Health Services Archive.

The following pages, which in their original format were handwritten or typed, describe the hospital treatment and social care support of my mother between July 1962 and August 1965. With a 4-month gap, they follow the birth of my third, and youngest brother, Leslie, on 23rd March 1962.

Strangely, her records abruptly cut off in August 1965 and I don't know why, for I know she underwent further treatment and hospitalisation after 1965.

For example, they omit her electroconvulsive therapy, her admittance to Edinburgh's Andrew

Duncan Clinic, or my memories of her addiction to Valium and Mogadon.

Except for redacting the names of professionals, the information presented remains as written in those 150 pages.

Family doctors, health visitors, social workers, nurses, psychiatrists, registrars, housing staff, and my parents originally wrote or typed these notes. They are sad, hard-hitting, and sometimes I can only best describe their words and content as vile. The language used then is certainly not what social workers and psychiatrists would use today.

I should add that as Lothian Health Services Archive originally released these documents to me for family history use only, I have therefore chosen to redact all names to protect their right to privacy. I also asked for permission to publish.

NOT SO SUNNY LEITH

GARY MILLAR

NOT SO SUNNY LEITH

It's Friday, March 23, 1962, and Madge, my mother, Mum, was 27. Gordon, my father, Dad, was 24. They married in March 1958. Something life-changing was about to hit, and it would hit hard.

On a lighter note, and purely as a point of interest, The Proclaimers, those Scottish folk rock musicians Charlie and Craig Reid, were born two weeks earlier. These twin brothers went on to not only 'walk 500 miles' they also released that 1988 hit mentioned in the previous chapter, and eventual Easter Road football terrace anthem, the aptly named 'Sunshine on Leith.'

In our not so sunny Leith, lying north of Edinburgh's city centre, the area was experiencing typical early spring weather. Temperatures were relatively mild for March - described in those days as 39° to 50° Fahrenheit, but as Mum would have later said, around 4° to 10° Celsius 'in new money.' On this eventful Friday, Edinburgh's skies were cloudy with some drizzle. Mum would have also described this weather as 'dreich.'

Against this backdrop, west of Easter Road, in our squalid, cold, drafty, and rodent infested flat, Mum gave birth to Leslie, her third child, my brother. I was two and a half years old and Norman, son number 2, was 18 months.

As Leslie entered this world to the sound of the guitar instrumental 'Wonderful Land' a joyful and hopeful guitar number that represented my parents' hopes and dreams for better times, those dreich 'dark shadows' had descended.

There had been initial relief following what had been a difficult pregnancy, followed by a realisation that he had entered this world in complete silence. He hadn't cried and Mum knew something was not quite right with what she later would describe as her 'wee doll!' We can only imagine the midwife's face, as she gently held onto this emerging miracle. With what we can only assume was a growing look of shock, she surely must have realised that something was very wrong with this newborn.

Until reading her case file, I did not know Mum had given birth to Leslie at home. In addition, I had not known, for example, that she had been evacuated during World War Two, or where she had been sent, or which schools she had attended and the subjects she liked (apparently, she loved 'cooking' - which is surprising as she used to burn everything). In addition, her notes tell me what she didn't like and how she felt growing up. Her file helped solve these mysteries and so much more!

So, please join me as you learn, in chronological

order, the trials and tribulations of three years in the life of Margaret Marjorie Millar, my Mum, Madge to her friends. Please call her Madge. She would have liked that, as sadly, her demons were many and, as a result, her friends few.

It's Friday, March 23, 1962. Not only had Mum's water broken, so had her heart.

Little did they know what they were about to face! With the benefit of accessing Mum's long forgotten case file, you are about to find out!

East William Street, Edinburgh

SILENCE

SILENCE

As though mimicking Leslie's silent world, Mum's health records are equally silent for the first four months of his fragile and shocking life. I can only imagine that no one beyond our family knew she was suffering. Surprisingly, there appear to be no health records between 23rd March and 26th July of that same year. I only stress this, as Leslie was born with major, and unknown, issues. Perhaps more surprisingly, despite significant health issues, her records are also missing for the final 37 years of her life.

I remember age old family stories suggesting that the medical profession thought Leslie may not live for long, and not beyond the end of 1962. Some in my family later added that perhaps some suggested he should not live at all. They thought it was unfair for him to live a life of suffering. I believe leaving him to die was discussed as an option and had he been born in hospital, I wonder if that would have been a more likely outcome?

As you will read, Edinburgh's Royal Infirmary Hospital first appears to have treated Mum as an outpatient in July 1962 – in Ward 3, a secure ward, following a cry for help!

In August of the same year, she willingly admitted

herself to Bangour Village Hospital as a voluntary patient (meaning she went there by her own choice and not forced or 'sectioned'). After her discharge from Bangour later in the same month, she had three subsequent, short-term voluntary admissions. Mum's last discharge from Bangour is recorded as being in March 1964 (though a psychiatric social worker, referred to as a 'P.S.W.' in the records, subsequently kept a watchful eye on Mum into 1965).

I should perhaps forewarn you that these following pages are, in places, distressing to read.

Helpfully, for me, with an advanced warning from Lothian Health Services, I received advice to find someone supportive whilst reading Mum's Case File. Especially when the content was particularly upsetting. Yet, I somehow managed to read all 150 pages multiple times. I eventually found the strength to speak aloud every single word and digitally store those to help tell this story. This certainly helped, but as expected, several of these notes and letters are quite shocking and many brought tears to my eyes.

As previously explained, I discovered the documents contained language that described patients in the 1960s in a way that differs greatly from what would be used in psychiatric care today. These papers, the notes you will now read, talk about Mum's feelings towards our family, social care, and the home situation of myself and my two brothers.

Sadly, according to the case files, Mum attempted suicide and health services admitted her to the secure ward (Ward 3) of the Royal Infirmary of Edinburgh on at least two of these occasions.

When I transcribed the information and where I could not read the text (because of handwriting issues or difficult to read faded and old sheets), I have inserted question marks to highlight any words or phrases that remain ineligible (fortunately there are very few).

For anyone interested in technology, I have used voice recognition software to store everything digitally. I used my own bespoke software to search for specific information and to re-sort everything into date order, so that it made better sense to me and to you.

Across those 150 pages, I found that there are 202 unique data items. This includes five letters from Mum's GPs; over 91 notes from hospital staff; her social workers recorded a further 69 notes and letters; Dad wrote five letters; and Mum only one. Others include exchanges between Edinburgh Corporation (city government), psychiatrists, and Registrars.

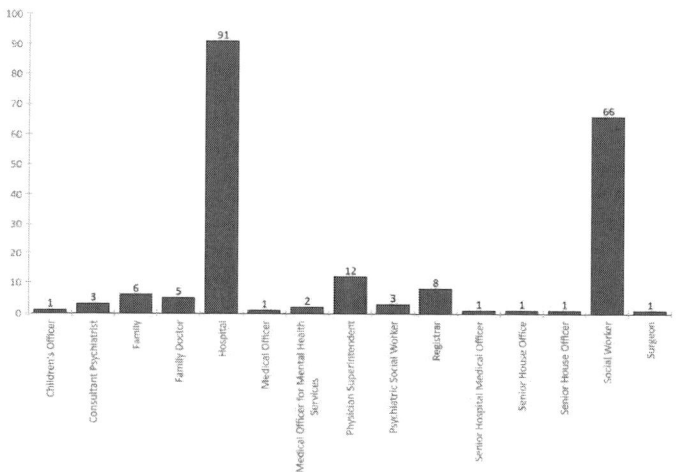

Mum's case file also mentions several prescribed drugs. Since I have no medical background, I researched and described, where necessary, what they are. The same goes for any clinical terms used. I have brought these details together in the 'Glossary of Medical Terms' section at the end of this book.

As I also had little knowledge about the institutions she had been admitted to, I conducted further research on those. However, please accept my apologies if I have made any mistakes with my rudimentary research.

This entire process has been a cathartic exercise, a cleansing, and, at times, a jaw dropping revelation. Some of the content is also, I admit, bland, but some of it has left me feeling either distressed or more intrigued.

However, despite the awful words used to describe my Mum and Dad (and others) I have, through this exercise, become more aware and forgiving of their failings, beatings, drinking, a litany of errors – and most importantly, their strengths!

Trivial things in Mum's health notes have meant a lot to me. I now have in my possession my only examples of notes written by Dad and the only one written by Mum – which in particular, later, had potentially significant consequences for her and our entire family. Also, two notes include content that no son wants to read about his mum, but I have included them for completeness - and with an apology to my dearly departed Mum!

These records have also solved many mysteries. Including one that has made me question my previous memories. One of those is about when I first met Leslie! As a result, I have put on hold the completion of a previous book, one that I have been writing for almost two years, until I weave this latest information into its existing 380 pages.

As of August 1965, at the conclusion of this book, one big mystery remains. In the years that followed, Mum continued to struggle with unanswered questions, desperate poverty, overdoses, suicide attempts, hysteria, domestic violence, abuse, self-doubt, unresolved blame, and a lifelong addiction to prescription drugs and alcohol.

It now appears that no similar hospital treatment records exist after those years. Yet I know for certain that a more devastating trauma would affect Mum's life and our own.

For these, I give you my apologies, as you will have to wait for some of those conclusions until you read my next book, *Silent Victims: Part 2* - planned for release in May 2025. I originally designed *Part 2* to be my first book about the impact of my youngest brother's birth on the wider family. Now being published after this book, it will describe what happened in the years following. The content of which will often be more shocking than any you will read in the following pages – and the pages you are about to read are horrifying, sad, and traumatic!

CASE NOTES – DAY 1

DAY 1

Next is a transcription of the first page recorded in Mum's case file from LHSA. It is a note from her GP requesting a confidential 'Request for Outpatient Consultation' to be delivered by the Jordanburn Nerve Hospital. It appears to be the first sign that Leslie, my brother, and her third child had been born with congenital defects four months previously.

Until reading this case note, I did not know she had lived in Newcastle or had tried to commit suicide there. I also now recognise that someone wrote it on the same date I first entered foster care – later corroborated by my own records.

Mum's destination, the Jordanburn Nerve Hospital, became part of the Royal Edinburgh Hospital for Mental and Nervous Disorders in 1929. The health service specifically designed Jordanburn to treat informal patients who could be admitted without formal legal procedures. We can trace the origins of Jordanburn back to the work done during World War I to help shell-shocked patients. This hospital played a crucial role in providing care for individuals experiencing mental health challenges, especially during a time when understanding and treating mental illnesses was developing.

This note also highlights the drugs that Mum's doctor had prescribed for her – including the sedative hypnotic barbiturates Amytal and Cyclobarbitone, antipsychotic medication Moditen, and iron supplement Ferrous Sulphate.

From this point forward, unless an explanation is needed, I have decided not to describe every single note. I think it is probably better that most do the talking for themselves.

GARY MILLAR

Thu, 26 July 1962

26.7.62
Name of patient: Margaret Millar
Age: 28

Address: 6 East William Street, Edinburgh, 7

History: This lady has not felt well since the birth of her third male child 4 months ago. Indeed, she did not feel well during the whole of her pregnancy which was complicated by rubella in the early weeks. Her baby was born with fairly severe congenital defects.

Mrs. Millar has been feeling 'at the end of her tether' during the last week. Things have got 'on top of her.' She sleeps badly, is tearful and she feels she could scream – if it were not for the children and the neighbours. She felt like this once before in 1958 before her first child was born. It was a Newcastle: She behaved 'foolishly' and took 14 barbiturate tablets. She does not feel 'quite bad enough to do that again.' Mrs. Millar has 2 boys of 3 and 2 years of age whom I have placed with foster parents today. I have also secured Leslie's admission to the Royal Sick Children's Hospital.

I assured Mrs. Millar I would try to obtain her early admission to hospital where she could have treatment for her 'nerves' and the 'heavy feeling on top of her head.'

Recent therapy has been Amytal gr (grain) T BD (twice daily), Moditen 1 mg BD (twice daily), Cyclobarbitone gr (grain) vt nocte (at night)

SILENT VICTIMS: PART ONE

and Ferrous Sulphate gr (grain) iii T.I.D. (three times a day).

Mrs. Millar lives with her husband in a two-room house. She is very happy with her husband. Housing is bad and inadequate. Her main problem has been how to cope with the four-month baby. Is the baby mentally defective? What will the future be? Is life worth living? To escape from it all?

Author's notes:

Drugs Administered: Amytal, Moditen, Cyclobarbitone, Ferrous Sulphate (please consult the 'Glossary of Medical Terms' at the end of this book for further information about each).

CASE NOTES – DAY 2

DAY 2

Because of lack of beds, mum did not enter Jordanburn Nerve Hospital as requested. Instead, she admitted herself as an outpatient to Edinburgh's Royal Infirmary Hospital. Her general admission record on this occasion includes seven handwritten pages that basically cover her life story to date, her feelings about family, and her current circumstances. Without seeing these, I would never have learned about her childhood, her teenage worries, and her schooling.

For me, these pages are a fascinating window into a previously hidden past. They allow me the benefit of travelling back in time to stand alongside, first my infant mum, and later her teenage version, to apple orchards and rolling pastures, to cooking classes and to happier times with aunts and grandparents.

However, the notes also paint a difficult, darker picture. One with demons, pleas for help, father issues, mother issues, loneliness, attempted suicide, difficult pregnancies, and intimacy problems. None of which I knew until reading these notes. They are shocking in their matter-of-fact briefness, and I am left wanting to know more. This includes wanting to see photographs from her childhood - there are none. Wanting to meet her small group of friends and listen to their stories of fun, laughter and first loves. I would love to stand alongside her in a cookery class and make scones together, see her happy face, and hear her laughing uncontrollably. I am left wondering whether she laughed and snorted loudly, the same as I do, when finding something funny? Sadly, we will never know!

Fri, 27 July 1962

Royal Infirmary Hospital Edinburgh (Outpatient Clinic): General Admission Record

27.7.62
```
General   admission   record.  With   a   note   from
███████████ that Mum was admitted to Bangour
on Saturday, 11th August 1962.
```

ROYAL INFIRMARY HOSPITAL

ROYAL INFIRMARY HOSPITAL

When she was 27, they initially treated Mum as an outpatient in the Royal Edinburgh Hospital (the Royal Infirmary of Edinburgh). In August of the same year, she then voluntarily admitted herself to Bangour Village Hospital. She returned to the Royal's secure ward (Ward 3) on 13th September 1962, having again threatened to kill herself and returned yet again on 8th November of that same year, this time having taken a small overdose of barbiturates. She returned on 29th March 1963, as a grave suicide risk, then on 31st May 1963 following a suicide attempt and in late February, 1964 following an argument with Dad.

1962
27/07/62 acute depression
13/09/62 threat of overdose
08/11/62 overdose

1963
29/03/63 suicide risk
31/05/63 suicide attempt

1964
28/02/64 made homeless
26/04/64 for sterilisation

In 1962, The Royal Infirmary of Edinburgh was one of the UK's leading medical institutions. Established in 1729, it had a long history of medical innovation and excellence. By 1962, the hospital was in Lauriston

Place, a site it had occupied since 1879. The facility earned a reputation as a centre for medical research and education because of its advanced medical practices, teaching, and strong association with the University of Edinburgh's Medical School. Renowned physicians and surgeons staffed the Royal Infirmary, providing a wide range of services, including specialised surgeries and treatments. Its infrastructure and medical technology were innovative for the time, contributing significantly to the development of modern medicine.

The hospital included psychiatric services as part of its comprehensive medical care, although they often separated psychiatric treatment from general medical care. The transition from more custodial care influenced the approach to psychiatric care towards more therapeutic and community-based treatments. Doctors might have treated patients like my Mum with a combination of methods, including psychotherapy, electroconvulsive therapy (ECT), and medications such as antipsychotics and antidepressants, which were relatively new and transforming the field.

The Royal Infirmary's psychiatric department took part in both inpatient and outpatient care, with a focus on more humane and rehabilitative practices compared to earlier decades. Staff included psychiatrists, psychologists, psychiatric nurses, and social workers, all contributing to a multi-disciplinary approach to mental health care. This is obvious from Mum's case file notes.

Research and education in psychiatry were integral parts of the department, benefiting from the hospital's association with the University of Edinburgh – who now manage these records. This connection helped advance psychiatric treatment and contributed to the training of medical students and professionals in the latest mental health practices.

The hospital later moved to its current location at Edinburgh's Little France in 2003.

SILENT VICTIMS: PART ONE

Page 1 - PREGNANCY & BIRTH

This page, the first of seven relating to this hospital admission, highlights that Mum had several health issues during her pregnancy with Leslie, including rubella, hydramnios, sickness, abdominal pain, and poor sleep.

Again, this page is the first time I learned she gave birth to Leslie at home, and it also appears to be the first recorded sign (in Mum's records) of his physical issues.

With some background information. Rubella, also known as German measles or three-day measles, is a contagious viral infection best known for its distinctive red rash. It is generally a mild disease in children and adults – but can cause serious complications if contracted by pregnant women. Hydramnios (also called polyhydramnios) is a condition in which there is too much amniotic fluid around the foetus. It occurs in about 1 percent of all pregnancies.

Although this note mentions Dad's perforated ulcer, I was previously under the mistaken impression that his first ulcer related issues did not take place until the 1970s. The note highlights that it was a longer-term health issue.

This page is also an early, yet understandably unknown hint of something much more serious, having affected Mum and Leslie during the pregnancy. I will explore this in greater detail in my next book, *Silent Victims: Part 2*.

SILENT VICTIMS: PART ONE

Fri, 27 July 1962

Royal Infirmary Hospital Edinburgh (Outpatient Clinic): Hospital Notes – Page 1

```
27.7.62
```
Cause of depression:
Malformed baby born four months ago.

Ordinary measles before pregnant general practitioner says rubella during early weeks during pregnancy causing sickness, abdominal pain and poor sleep.

Couldn't sit properly.

Had hydramnios.

Sickness during day. Sometimes all day and at night throughout the pregnancy. Not in hospital at any time. Delivered at home. Just three months before birth, husband in hospital with a perforated ulcer. No help at home. Attended at house by ▮▮▮▮▮▮▮. Midwife delivered the baby.

Baby boy born without ears defective sight. No other defects yet found. Difficult to wean at first. Much vomiting, now stopped.

Page 2 – SHE LEFT ME

Mum's paternal Grandfather, Alexander, was born in 1888, and died in 1955 from natural causes and Coronary Thrombosis. Her paternal Grandmother, Margaret Marjory, was born in 1889, and died in 1937. I discovered she died from Chronic Bronchitis and Myocarditis (a disease that causes inflammation of the heart muscle).

Archie or Archibald, her father, was born in 1912. Until reading this page, I had absolutely no recollection of his disabilities. I am not surprised by Mum's comments about her father. Others in our family have corroborated and heavily criticised his bitterness and behavioural issues.

Maggie, her mother, of whom 'he never speaks' was born in 1914, married in 1934 and disappeared in 1936. I did not know her whereabouts until the conclusion of some of my family's research in 2010. I discovered she had died in Dunfermline in 1984 from a cerebrovascular accident (a stroke) and atherosclerosis (a condition where the arteries become narrowed and hardened because of a buildup of plaque in the artery wall). During that research, I was also pleasantly surprised to learn that her mother, my gran, had given birth to five additional children between the years

1939 and 1951. In fact, I had the pleasure of meeting and becoming friends with two brothers, Uncles Eddie and William. William, although unwell, is still with us.

Mum never met her mother after she disappeared in 1936 and, of course, also never met those five half-siblings. This is heartbreaking, as I know she, an only child, always wanted a brother and a sister or two. Most of all, she really wanted her Mum!

Royal Infirmary Hospital Edinburgh (Outpatient Clinic): Hospital Notes – Page 2

27.7.62

Grandfather: Lamplighter. Died at 67 from thrombosis.

Grandmother: died young - 'heart trouble'

Father: 50. A & W. 'Born a cripple.' Legs like match sticks. Club foot. Belongs to Spastics Club. Mentally weak. Works in Morningside Laundry.

Mother: 'He never speaks of her.' She left the house when I was 2 and a half years old. Doesn't know age or whereabouts.

No brothers or sisters – brought up by father's sister. Doesn't get on with father - didn't see eye to eye. Hard man to get on with – 'bitter against all the world.'

Born in Edinburgh. At 2 1/2 mother left. Other men. 'Lots of stories.' Brought up in grandparents' house, father lived there. Aunts and uncles all got married. Left with grandparents and father. Got on with grandfather.

Unhappy as child – didn't play with children. Couldn't understand why she didn't have mother or go out with parents like other children.

SILENT VICTIMS: PART ONE

Page 3 – MOTHERHOOD

Her Mum 'Maggie' disappeared in 1936, and my Mum and I believe her dad 'Archie,' my Grandad, never saw her again. Elizabeth 'Auntie Bet' Hanley, sister to Archie, became her much loved surrogate. In later years, I learned my 'Auntie Betty' (I never called her Auntie Bet) enjoyed reading the tea leaves and revelled in her notoriety as a fortune teller – or as we say in Scotland, a 'Spey-wife.'

Mum adored her 'Auntie Bet.' She learned much from her, and as a result was also often called a 'Spey-wife.' Mum not only learned to read the tea leaves, but she was also, sometimes scarily, very capable of reading people.

In the years that follow these 150 pages, whilst Mum was in hospital, Auntie Bet's daughter Sandra, Mum's cousin, and her husband Tam, often looked after both me and my brother Norman. Today, we would call her a 'kinship carer,' although in her case, I believe she always took care of us unofficially. It seems Social Services never knew we spent months living a fun, yet somewhat dysfunctional life with her and her family in Granton.

Although I never learned to read tea leaves, I instead learned that 'Auntie' Sandra was fun. She loved Elvis, short skirts, cigarettes, partying, and alcohol. As a child, she was an award-winning Scottish sword dancer. So, if she didn't play Elvis hits on her Dansette record player, or later on her new fancy stereogram, her alternative music of choice included the bagpipes, Scottish drums, Andy Stewart, or 'legend in his own lunchtime' Mr Sydney Devine.

There was something special about Auntie Betty and her family, and I love them for always supporting Mum.

SILENT VICTIMS: PART ONE

Royal Infirmary Hospital Edinburgh (Outpatient Clinic): Hospital Notes – Page 3

```
  27.7.62
Elizabeth Hanley (patients Aunt)
I always wanted to be a mother. Always
?????? (word ineligible) Couldn't settle
down.

Father born with club foot. Not spastic. One
foot smaller - normal shoes.

Marriage - happy in own way. Seems to think
husband could do a lot more. We think he
does a lot - looking after children - can do
a wash. Runs a happy household whenever I
go.

Baby an hour to feed. Doesn't look right.
```

SILENT VICTIMS: PART ONE

Page 4 – LEAVING HOME

Mum's grandfather's house was at 6 Stenhouse Drive, Edinburgh. Stenhouse lies to the west of the City Centre, next to Whitson and Saughton Mains and close to Broomhouse and Chesser. This had been the family home since the 1930s. Except for her wartime evacuation, it had been Mum's home until her beloved grandfather's death in 1955.

Auntie Bet's marital home was at 4 Easter Drylaw Bank, being an area in the northwest of Edinburgh, between Blackhall and Granton. I remember many happy memories of our visits there. Once together, she and Mum loved to smoke, drink, dance and giggle a lot. Although, I have to say, Auntie Bet's husband, a stonemason, never appeared the giggling type. He was what you could call a 'dour man's man.'

Dad's brewery job was at Archibald Campbell, Hope & King Ltd, Argyle Brewery, Chambers Street, Edinburgh. Which is ironic, knowing Dad's later issues with alcohol.

The comment about Newcastle has surprised me. I did not know, until reading these notes, that Dad had left Mum following their marriage and that once she found out where he had disappeared to, they had lived for a short while in Newcastle.

Finally, I had contemplated not including the social

worker's comments about their intimacy, or lack of it, but I have done so for completeness! My heavenly apologies to both.

SILENT VICTIMS: PART ONE

Royal Infirmary Hospital Edinburgh (Outpatient Clinic): Hospital Notes – Page 4

```
27.7.62
```
Left home at 21 when grandfather died.

Lived with Aunt for two months in 2 rooms, like married. House taken of them because in grandfather's name. Didn't get on with father – 'felt need to get out.'

Marriage

1958 – married at 24 years. Husband 21 years. Husband works in brewery.

Just after married, moved to Newcastle for six months. Unhappy there - husband left me just after we were married - changing jobs, didn't tell me. Went away – joined him. When I found him, we didn't get on. I was miserable and homesick.

Sexual intercourse was OK at beginning – later he was too tired often. Often only once a month. Since last baby, 'I haven't felt like it,' and sometimes a row if she doesn't reach climax.

Page 5 – FIRST SUICIDE ATTEMPT

This is a new and shocking revelation. Until these notes, I did not know Mum had tried to take her own life in Newcastle. This happened prior to my birth.

She must have been struggling so much after the revelations from Newcastle described on the previous page.

I am also picking up some sense of Dad's immaturity (as later described in these notes), where (in my opinion), this page highlights the fact that 'he didn't realise responsibilities.' I presume that once married, he changed jobs, moved to Newcastle and chose not to tell his new wife!

At least we can be reassured from these notes that he didn't leave to 'go off with other women!'

I now wish I had more information about their time in Newcastle, and I really do hope Mum received professional help. Instead, as I suspect, they simply swept this sad episode under the carpet on their return to Edinburgh. Maybe her first pregnancy was her only therapy.

In fact, I now wonder if my parents conceived me in Newcastle. I think it is relevant for me to ponder whether I resulted from her cries for help, or for attention? Was my birth a result of them both seeking a mutual forgiveness? Of course we will now never know. But at least I know from reading this page that she was 'happy with first child.'

Learning that Norman wasn't planned is disheartening. Although I must stress that despite this comment, Norman was most definitely loved following his birth. However, I know he has other views based on his own later experiences.

Royal Infirmary Hospital Edinburgh (Outpatient Clinic): Hospital Notes – Page 3

27.7.62

At first, he didn't realise responsibilities – didn't go off with other women.

Tried to commit suicide - took 14 barbiturate tablets. Stomach pump – didn't keep her in. Husband didn't care about it. We were getting on each other nerves so much. I couldn't do it again, couldn't stand stomach pump.

Children:
Gary, 3 in one week
Norman, 2 in October
Leslie, 4 months

First pregnancies OK – didn't want another baby. Anyway, not so soon – have had enough. Using vaginal tabs as contraceptives. Now to go to clinic.

Happy with first child – always wanted someone to love. 2nd child not planned.

Page 6 – SMALL ROOM & KITCHEN

It was shocking to learn about Mum's attempted suicide in Newcastle in 1958 and here she was in 1962, still harbouring thoughts of ending her life.

We lived at 6 East William Street, Edinburgh. Two small rooms, one of which was called 'a room and kitchen' and the other a bedroom. In between arguing 'an awful lot,' Mum and Dad slept in an alcove behind a curtain, in this room and kitchen. My brother Norman and I (and, at times, Grandad Archie) slept in the only cramped and damp bedroom. I clearly remember how uncomfortable my mattress was, hard, and 'jaggy' against my baby skin. The mattress was jaggy, not just because of the horsehair filling, but also because some of the pocket springs were broken.

Our compact kitchen included a stainless-steel sink and an old black lead 'grate' or range – for cooking food, hot water, drying the washing and heating the room. Once a week, either Mum or Dad bathed me in a white ceramic coated tin bath with a cobalt blue rim and a rusting bite-sized chip. The tub being placed on top of the stainless-steel sink drainer, filled with hot water from pans and kettle boiled on the black grate. They would lift me in for my weekly wash. I can still remember the rusting chip, framed either side by a thin blue stripe.

Our outdoor toilet was on the building's external landing and designed for all to share. Residents tore up newspaper strips and stuck them on a large nail to use as toilet paper. If we were lucky enough to have some spare cash, my parents would substitute the newspaper cuttings with IZAL Medicated (and impractically shiny) Toilet Sheets.

SILENT VICTIMS: PART ONE

Royal Infirmary Hospital Edinburgh (Outpatient Clinic): Hospital Notes – Page 6

27.7.62
General complaints – July depressed, crying and screaming. Very irritable – children's noise, etc. Can sleep now with tablets for one week before that 'too restless.' Difficulty in getting off, hardly sleeping at all. Waking 6 AM. Very poor appetite, feels thinner. No interest in anything. Suicidal thoughts.

Menstruation 10-21/18-20 normal flow. Before pregnancy 9/20 1-24.

Husband, very helpful, didn't understand before – he does now. Got annoyed with her, lost his temper. Quote 'Quarrel an awful lot,' but generally fond and get on with each other. 'Fond of home and children, but home too small.'

House. Small room and kitchen. All sleep in same room. Living there for three years. Corporation list – don't get house till eldest child 10 – now 3. No place for children to play. This afternoon to foster parents.

SILENT VICTIMS: PART ONE

Page 7 – HER CHILDHOOD

I knew none of these details until reading Mum's case file. I did not know of her wartime evacuation or her fear of the dark and her long-term issues with bed wetting.

Scottish children, like Mum, were first evacuated during World War II in September 1939, shortly after the outbreak of the war. This was part of the government's plan to protect civilians, especially children, from the expected air raids and bombings by Nazi Germany. The evacuation aimed to move children, along with pregnant women, mothers with young children, and disabled people, from urban areas and industrial cities to safer locations in the countryside. We learn here that Mum's safe zone was St Boswells, a village on the south side of the River Tweed, described as a land of rolling pastures and apple orchards in the Scottish Borders, about 1 mile southeast of Newtown St Boswells on the A68 road. However, I believe the term used 'St Newlands' is incorrect and instead should have been 'Newtown St Boswells?' Mum may have simply made an error in remembering from when she was only 5 years old.

Her first school, Edinburgh's Stenhouse Primary School, is a non-denominational school built in 1930, arranged around a central courtyard containing a large garden and nature area. Her secondary school was based in Saughton, in a suburb to the west of Edinburgh, bordering Broomhouse, Stenhouse, Longstone and Carrick Knowe. Interestingly, in Lowland Scots, a 'sauch' is a willow – and is my favourite tree. Saughton School was renamed Carrickvale School. Interestingly, because Saughton Prison was nearby, Carrickvale School was also known as 'Carrickjail.'

SILENT VICTIMS: PART ONE

Royal Infirmary Hospital Edinburgh (Outpatient Clinic): Hospital Notes – Page 7

Children okay. Frightened of dark - wet bed until married.

Evacuated at five years old to St Boswells and St Newlands. Sent home for wetting the bed – very bad then. Different schools. Away about two years.

Stenhouse 7 - 12.
Saughton School (Carrickvale Secondary) 12 - 15.
Left school at 15.

Didn't like school 'wasn't very bright.' Cooking best subject. Didn't like games 'never seemed well enough' – nothing particularly wrong – 'under the weather all the time.' Only one or two friends. OK with teachers.

Jobs (age 15 - 17)
Domestic service – 1 month. Too much work.
Shop – bakers – 6 months. Couldn't stick hours.
Domestic service – 18 months. On call any time. Not enough sleep.

Jobs (age 18 - 24)
Laundry. Different laundries till getting married at age 24.

Jobs (age 25)
Selling catalogues for 6 months, till expecting second child. Needed money.

GARY MILLAR

Sat, 28 July 1962

Jordanburn Nerve Hospital: Letter to GP

▇▇▇▇▇▇▇▇▇▇,
16 Windsor Street,
EDINBURGH

Dear ▇▇▇▇▇▇▇▇,

Thank you for your very full and helpful letter about Mrs. Margaret Millar, whom I saw with her husband yesterday. Unfortunately, I simply cannot find a bed for her as we are so very busy, but I have put her name on the waiting list for admission and shall try to carry her along as an out-patient in the meantime, seeing her on Fridays.

She thinks she can carry on at home, especially as you have relieved her of the responsibility of the three children. I arranged with her and with her husband that she should not be alone all day but should go to her mother-in-law or to her aunt or other relatives regularly Monday to Friday. I cannot improve upon the drugs you are giving her, but I asked the husband to make sure that he kept them.

Yours sincerely,
▇▇▇▇▇▇▇

BANGOUR VILLAGE HOSPITAL

BANGOUR VILLAGE HOSPITAL

Bangour Village Hospital was a pioneering psychiatric hospital designed in the early 20th century with a village layout to create a more therapeutic environment for patients. Built in 1906, it served important roles during both World Wars but declined with changes in mental health care practices. The site now remains largely abandoned, though there are ongoing discussions about its redevelopment.

Initially, Bangour Village Hospital was intended as a mental asylum to ease overcrowding at existing facilities.

The hospital was laid out like a village, with

individual villas for patients, a church, recreational facilities, staff housing, and its own farm. This design aimed to create a more humane and therapeutic environment for patients.

Mum entered Bangour Village Hospital on Saturday, 11 August 1962, and left on Wednesday, 22 August 1962.

Thu, 9 August 1962

Bangour Village Hospital: Letter to Mum about a bed becoming available.

```
                                  9th August, 1962.

                              Mrs. Margaret Millar,
                               6 East William Street,
                                              LEITH
```

Dear Mrs. Millar,

As there is now a bed available for you, will you please come for admission to Ward 2, Bangour Village Hospital, Broxburn, on Saturday, 11th August, 1962, about 10 a.m.

Yours sincerely,
███████████,
Consultant Psychiatrist.

SILENT VICTIMS: PART ONE

Sat, 11 August 1962

Bangour Village Hospital (Ward 2): Admission Notes – includes possessions list, height, height, temperature, pulse and respn.

```
11.08.62
IN POSSESSION ON ADMISSION

   1 Raincoat
   1 Headscarf
   1 Pr Shoes
   1 Skirt
   1 Jumper
   1 Bra
   1 Girdle
   1 Underskirt
   1 Pr Pants
   3 Nightdresses
   1 Dressing Gown
   1 Pr Slippers
   1 Handbag
   1 Shopper
   1 Pr Stockings
   1 Rain mate
   Top Dentures
   1 Wedding Ring
   1 Eternity Ring
   1 Bracelet Watch
   2 Bracelets
   Purse containing £3-1-6 1/2.

   Height: 5'5"
   Weight: 8st 8Ibs
```

GARY MILLAR

Sat, 11 August 1962

Bangour Village Hospital (Ward 2): Admission Notes on 11.08.62

FAMILY HISTORY
Mother left father of patient age 2 1/2, and no contact since. Patient was brought up mainly by a series of aunts, and in childhood did not get on at all well with her father, although relations have improved recently. At school she resented being different from the other children in family circumstances. She is an only child, and there is no known family history of mental disorder.

PREVIOUS HISTORY
Born and brought up in Edinburgh. At school she was an average scholar and got on well enough with her classmates. After leaving school at 15 she was in a succession of short-lived jobs, usually leaving because she was 'not robust enough', although she cannot describe any specific illness. Since marriage four years ago, she has not had an outside job. Her husband is a labourer in a brewery, and two years her junior. Since marriage they have lived in a squalid and overcrowded room and kitchen, which she hates, but all efforts to speed her progress up the new housing list have been unsuccessful. They have three children, all boys, age 3, 2 and 4 months. The youngest child unfortunately has an uncertain amount of physical malformations and may also be somewhat mentally retarded and is at present being investigated in the Sick

SILENT VICTIMS: PART ONE

Children's Hospital (patient had ordinary measles early in the pregnancy but this may be of no significance). Neither of the two youngest children were really wanted or planned, because of the poor housing situation, but having been born they have been wholly accepted by the patient. Her relations with her husband are usually satisfactory, although the initial period of adjustment was rather prolonged.

She is usually an active cheerful person, but she has found her young family very trying and gets no time to enjoy any social life, although she claims to have plenty of friends.

All the births have been quite eventful, but during her last pregnancy she had severe bouts of sickness. Following the birth of her second child, she felt depressed, with symptoms similar to those of the present illness, for about a month before she improved spontaneously. She has had no physical illnesses of note.

PRESENT ILLNESS
Since the birth of her third child some four months ago she has felt consistently depressed (no diurnal variation). This has been getting worse and during the past few weeks she has been sleeping badly (rhythm vague), finding great difficulty in concentrating, been markedly irritable, suffered from frontal and occipital headaches, and experienced dizziness on rising in the morning. She feels that all this has been precipitated by her many worries, i.e. anxiety concerning her child's deformities with no knowledge of how much more is to be detected yet; inability to cope with her family in her most unsatisfactory domestic situation, and anxiety about her husband's health (operation

for perforated peptic ulcer and appendicitis seven months ago). More recently she has felt a little better on some new pills prescribed for her (Tofranil).

STATE IN ADMISSION
A pale thin haggard woman who is prematurely aged. She is rather tense and appears only moderately depressed. She impresses as being of rather low intelligence.

FORMULATION
A woman probably of limited intelligence and inadequate (to her duties) personality who is suffering from a second depression in the puerperium. This depression seems to be more of a reactive nature to her many very real worries rather than a true puerperal psychosis.

SILENT VICTIMS: PART ONE

Sat, 11 August 1962 - Wed, 22 August 1962

Bangour Village Hospital (Ward 2): Ward Notes

11.8.62
Admitted from home at 11 am. Has been very depressed since the birth of her baby. Appears to be settling down. Commenced Sodium Amytal nocte.

12.8.62
Has had a comfortable day, but still remains depressed.

17.8.62
At gynaecology clinic for routine examination in the a.m. Comfortable day. Meals taken well.

18.8.62
Much brighter. Condition improved greatly.

20.8.62
Progress steadily improving. More active. Taking part in ward routine. Going for walks with other patients and going to occupational therapy department.

22.8.62
Discharged home today.

DEPRESSION

MUM'S DEPRESSION

This letter to her GP confirms that Mum's recent admission to Bangour Village Hospital involved a prescription of Tofranil, Melleril, and Sodium Amytal (for further details about these drugs, please consult the 'Glossary of Medical Terms' at the end of this book).

It also highlights and discounts **puerperal depressive psychosis**. This condition, known as postpartum psychosis, is said to be a severe mental illness that can occur in women after childbirth. It is a rare but serious condition characterised by an acute onset of psychotic symptoms, typically within the first two weeks following delivery.

Instead, Mum may have a depression reactive to various difficulties. This is also referred to as **reactive depression** or situational depression, and it is a type of depressive disorder that occurs in response to specific life stressors or adverse events. Unlike major depressive disorder, which can occur without an identifiable trigger, reactive depression is associated with external circumstances or challenges.

SILENT VICTIMS: PART ONE

Wed, 22 August 1962

Bangour Village Hospital: Letter to GP about discharge from hospital and drugs administered during admission.

22nd August, 1962

███████████,
16 Windsor Street,
EDINBURGH.

Dear ███████████,

Mrs. MARGARET MILLAR, 6, E. William Street, Edinburgh.

This patient, who was admitted on 13th August, 1962 is being discharged today, 22nd August, 1962.

You may recall that she has complained of depressive symptoms since the birth of her third child, about four months ago. Her home background is most unsatisfactory and there is no doubt that she finds herself unable to cope with three young children in much difficult surroundings. In fact, she had similar depressive symptoms for about a month following the birth of the second child, but these cleared spontaneously. A further factor with her present illness is that her latest child appeared to have a number of physical deformities which are causing Mrs. Millar considerable anxiety.

While a patient here, she has been treated with much the same medication as she had before admission namely Tofranil, 25 mgm. G.i.d. and Melleril, 25 mgm, t.i.d., with Sodium Amytal, gr. 3 at night. Almost from admission she has felt very much better, and I do not consider her illness to be a true puerperal depressive psychosis, but rather a depression reactive to her various difficulties. She is very keen to go off at the end of this week on an arranged holiday with her husband and I had no objections to this plan. I would suggest that she be continued, in the meantime, on the above medication.

Yours sincerely,

███████████,
Registrar.

SILENT VICTIMS: PART ONE

Wed, 29 August 1962

Bangour Village Hospital: Letter to Mum confirming appointment on Monday, 03.09.62 at 3 p.m.

```
                              Mrs. Margaret Millar,
                              6, East William Street,
                                           EDINBURGH.

  Dear Mrs. Millar,

I could see you at my clinic at the Sighthill
Health Centre, Edinburgh on MONDAY 3rd September
at 3 p.m. I hope this will be convenient for
you.

  Yours faithfully,
  ███████████ ,
  Physician Superintendent.
```

Author's Notes:
On 15th May 1953, Sighthill Health Centre became the first health centre in Scotland and the second to be built in the UK.

Mon, 3 September 1962

Royal Infirmary Hospital Edinburgh (Outpatient Clinic): Hospital Notes

3.9.62

Did not go on holiday because baby was ill.

Sleeping well. Has slept two nights without tablets.

Occasional shaky spells yesterday all day.

Spirits not too bad.

Wee one has a bad cold.

No crying fits. On the whole rather better.

ATTEMPTED SUICIDE

ATTEMPTED SUICIDE

Having again threatened to kill herself, in hysteria, Mum was admitted to the Royal Infirmary Hospital secure ward (Ward 3) on either 13th or 14th September (the records include these two dates as dates of admission, although I am leaning more towards late evening of the 13th as a more accurate timing).

She left the hospital on the 18th.

In later notes from this period, it reads as though she may have also been in fear of again being pregnant. **See note:** 18/09/62.

Fri, 14 September 1962

Royal Infirmary Hospital Edinburgh (Outpatient Clinic): Admission record - 14.09.62

```
Date of Admission: 14.09.62 following Hysteria -
Suicidal Risk
```

Tue, 18 September 1962

Royal Infirmary Hospital Edinburgh (Outpatient Clinic): Discharge record - 18.09.62

```
Date of Discharge: 18.09.62 following treatment
for Hysteria - Suicidal Risk
```

Tue, 18 September 1962

Royal Infirmary Hospital Edinburgh: Covering letter to Hospital Psychiatrist attaching copy of Ward 3 report - 18.09.62.

```
Department of Psychological Medicine,
2 George Square,
Edinburgh 9.
```

18th September, 1962.

Bangour Hospital,
West Lothian.

Dear ███████,

We had Marjorie Millar with us briefly until today and I enclose a copy of her Ward 3 report in case it is any use to you.

At one time I thought we were going to have to recommend another spell as an in-patient because she was so agitated. However, the spontaneous occurrence of a period has relieved her of her chief worry, and she is now much better.

Yours sincerely,

███████,
Consultant Psychiatrist.

AGITATED DEPRESSION

AGITATED DEPRESSION

These notes indicate Mum was believed to suffer from agitated depression, also known as agitated major depressive disorder (MDD). This, I understand, is a subtype of depression characterised by symptoms, as its name implies, of both depression and agitation. It represents a complex and challenging form of depressive illness that can significantly affect an individual's functioning and quality of life.

Symptoms: Individuals, like my Mum, with agitated depression, experience the typical symptoms of depression, including persistent feelings of sadness, hopelessness, and worthlessness. They may also exhibit a loss of interest or pleasure in activities they once enjoyed. Restlessness, irritability, and difficulty sitting still, rapid speech, racing thoughts, and an inability to concentrate or focus also characterised it. Other symptoms may include insomnia or disrupted sleep patterns, changes in appetite or weight, fatigue, and physical tension or discomfort.

I am upset to learn for the first time, from these notes, that Mum had a nervous breakdown when she was only 17 years old.

SILENT VICTIMS: PART ONE

Tue, 18 September 1962

Royal Infirmary Hospital Edinburgh (Ward 3): Psychiatrist Notes from 14.09.62

```
Department of Psychological Medicine,
Royal Infirmary,
Edinburgh

Marjorie Millar
6 East William Street,
Edinburgh

27 years

Ward 3
14.9.62
```

GP: ███████████, 16 Windsor Street, Edinburgh.

Married, aged 27, admitted on 13th September, having threatened to kill herself.

Three weeks before hand she had been discharged from Bangour after a three weeks spell of reactive depression. Circumstances conspired to precipitate this attempt. On the day before it her five months old youngest child's deafness was confirmed to her, and she saw him for the first time with a hearing aid. Also, she was a little overdue and feared that she was pregnant. On the evening before admission, she seemed unnaturally quiet, went to bed at eleven and about midnight began to get agitated, giggling and saying she would find and take tablets.

GARY MILLAR

She had a nervous breakdown when she was 17 and in 1958, she attempted suicide in Newcastle.

On examination on 14th September, she showed typical features of agitated depression. Seen again today she was considerably improved. The fact that menstruation has supervened is no doubt largely responsible for this.

Diagnosis: Agitated depression.

Disposal: She should keep her out-patient follow-up appointment with ▮▮▮▮▮▮ in a week's time.

▮▮▮▮▮▮,
Consultant Psychiatrist,

18 September 1962.

SILENT VICTIMS: PART ONE

Mon, 24 September 1962

Outpatient Notes - 24.09.62

24.9.62
Baby has been very ill with colds. Bronchitis.

Losing weight and not thriving. Don't think hearing aid will work.

Staying with mother-in-law – Mrs. Millar, 1 Burdiehouse Avenue.

Has other children home now.

Agreed that I speak to ███████████.

BLOOD WORK

BLOOD WORK

Although I have explained these terms in the 'Glossary of Medical Terms' section at the end of this book, it is useful to better understand how the results affected Mum.

An oxygen saturation level of 81% is lower than the normal range and may show hypoxaemia, which means there is a reduced level of oxygen in the blood. Many factors can cause Hypoxaemia, including lung diseases, heart conditions, altitude, or certain medical emergencies. If someone has an oxygen saturation level of 81%, it's essential to seek medical attention promptly to determine the cause and receive treatment. Severe or prolonged hypoxaemia can lead to serious complications and requires immediate intervention.

A P.C.V. of 33% may be within the normal range for some populations, but it could also show conditions, such as anaemia or dehydration.

An M.C.H.C. value of 36% would be considered within the normal range. However, abnormalities in levels can sometimes show certain health conditions, such as anaemia or hemoglobinopathies. It's important to interpret M.C.H.C. results with other blood tests and clinical findings to determine their significance.

SILENT VICTIMS: PART ONE

Tue, 25 September 1962

Royal Infirmary Hospital Edinburgh (Ward 31): Letter to GP about attempted suicide, blood census, including a copy of psychiatric report.

```
                                    Ward 31,
                         The Royal infirmary,
                              Edinburgh, 3.

                         September, 25th 1962


                              16 Windsor Street,
                                      EDINBURGH.
```

Dear ███████,

Re: Mrs. MARGARET MILLAR, (27) 6, East William Street, Edinburgh.

Your patient was admitted to Ward 3 under the care of ███████ on 14.9.62 threatening to attempt suicide.

On admission she was conscious and somewhat upset, clinical examination failed to reveal any abnormality, and she settled well with routine care. She was noted to be somewhat pale. A blood census which was carried out showed an Hb. Of 81%, P.C.V. 33%, M.C.H.C. 36% E.S.R. 7 mm in the first hour, W.B.C. 8,300. Though her Hb. Is not unduly low the M.C.H.C. is raised and it is possible that this patient may be suffering from megaloblastic anaemia. If you are concerned about her from this aspect, we would be happy to investigate it further and will be pleased to see her in Ward 31 on Wednesday morning by appointment.

In view of her story of recent psychiatric care, she was seen by the psychiatrist here ▮▮▮▮ who diagnosed agitated depression, and a full copy of his report is enclosed for your information. She was discharged home on 18.9.62.

Yours sincerely,

(Signed) ▮▮▮▮,
Senior House Officer.

Copy to Bangour.

SILENT VICTIMS: PART ONE

Mon, 8 October 1962

Outpatient Notes - 08.10.62

```
8.10.62
```
Wee one still in hospital but gaining. Getting on fine now.

Back in own house and finding it very crowded.

Hoping to get others into the nursery.

Managing housework rituals alright.

Spoke to ███████████.

Sun, 28 October 1962

Outpatient Notes - 28.10.62

28.10.62
Has baby boy home now. She forgets to take tablets and feels sick.

Doing without sleeping tablets.

Has a bad cold.

Worried about baby. Afraid of his not gaining.

Rather better on the whole.

OVERDOSE

OVERDOSE

They admitted Mum to Royal Infirmary Hospital's secure ward (Ward 3) in Edinburgh following a Sodium Amytal overdose. This unfortunate incident followed a violent disagreement with Dad. A letter from her GP to Jordanburn Nerve Hospital on 12th November 1962 notes that she neglects her children.

The doctors discharged her the following day (the 9th).

SILENT VICTIMS: PART ONE

Thu, 8 November 1962

Royal Infirmary Hospital Edinburgh (Outpatient Clinic): Admission record on 08.11.62 following prescribed drug overdose

```
8.11.62
   Date of Admission: 08.11.62 following Sodium
Amytal overdose.
```

Fri, 9 November 1962

Royal Infirmary Hospital Edinburgh (Ward 3): Discharge record

```
9.11.62
Date of Discharge: 09.11.62 following treatment
for Sodium Amytal overdose.
```

GARY MILLAR

Mon, 12 November 1962

Royal Infirmary Hospital Edinburgh: Letter to GP about Mum's admittance to Ward 3 on 8.11.62

```
                                     Ward 31,
                            The Royal infirmary,
                                  Edinburgh, 3.

                                 Nov, 12th 1962
                              ▉▉▉▉▉▉▉▉▉▉▉▉▉▉
                              16 Windsor Street,
                                    EDINBURGH 7.
```

Dear ▉▉▉▉▉▉▉▉▉▉,

Re: Mrs. MARGARET MILLAR, (27) 6, East William Street, Edinburgh.

You are patient was admitted to Ward 3 under the care of ▉▉▉▉▉▉▉▉▉▉ on 8.11.62 having taken a small overdose of barbiturates.

On admission she was conscious but drowsy and routine physical examination revealed no abnormalities.
She is a known depressive and is currently attending ▉▉▉▉▉▉▉▉▉▉ at Sighthill and has agreed to keep her appointment with him on 12.11.62. She was discharged home on 9.11.62.

```
    Yours sincerely,
    ▉▉▉▉▉▉▉▉▉▉,
    Senior House Officer.

    Copy to ▉▉▉▉▉▉▉▉▉▉, Sighthill.
```

SILENT VICTIMS: PART ONE

Mon, 12 November 1962

Royal Infirmary Hospital Edinburgh (Outpatient Clinic): Hospital Notes

```
12.11.62
```
Having rows with husband.

Landed in Ward 3 on Thursday. Out on Friday.

Crying a lot. Wants to come back in – she thinks.

Has not been taking her Tofranil.

Has fallen out with mother-in-law over it all.

Mon, 12 November 1962

GP: Letter to Jordanburn Nerve Hospital about Mum's state of mind

```
                                    16 Windsor Street,
                                        Edinburgh, 7
```

Dear ▮▮▮▮▮,

Mrs Margaret Millar was in Ward 3 from 6/11/62 to 9/11/62 as a result of Sodium Amytal overdosage.

She is very unhappy and depressed. I don't think I have seen her quite so ill before and so full of suicidal intent.

The children are neglected and there is violent disagreement with the husband.

I think it is now a question of Mrs. Millar going back into hospital or making a more determined attempt at a very early date.

Yours sincerely,

▮▮▮▮▮.

SILENT VICTIMS: PART ONE

Thu, 15 November 1962

Edinburgh Corporation: Letter to Physician Superintendent at Bangour Hospital about 'housing list' points

```
                            Edinburgh Corporation
                            Public Health Department
                                  Johnston Terrace,
                                       Edinburgh 1

                            15th November, 1962.


                                      ███████████,
                            Physician Superintendent,
                                   Bangour Hospital,
                                          Broxburn,
                                      West Lothian.
```

Dear ███████████,

Re. Mrs. Millar, 6 East William Street, Edinburgh, 7.

I am sorry there has been a little delay in writing to you about this patient, whom you referred on October 11. I've visited this lady with the health visitor and, subsequently, took up her case with our sanitary department and with the house-letting department. We have now given her points for overcrowding and also the medical points which we can give for medical priority. This should help her case considerably and I do hope that the housing department will be able to give her a house soon, particularly in view of the fact that, I understand, she has been admitted to Ward 3 of the Royal Infirmary following attempted suicide.

Yours sincerely,
████████ ██████,
Medical Officer for Mental Health Services.

SILENT VICTIMS: PART ONE

Fri, 16 November 1962

Bangour Village Hospital: Letter reply from Physician Superintendent about 'housing list' points to Medical Officer for Mental Health Services at Edinburgh Corporation.

```
                                16th November, 1962.

                        ███████████,
        Medical Officer for Mental Health Services,
                        Public Health Department,
                            Johnston Terrace,
                              EDINBURGH, 1

Dear ███████████,

Mrs. Millar, 6 East William Street, Edinburgh.

Thank you for letting me know about Mrs. Millar.
I saw her on Monday, and she told me that she
had been allocated extra points. As you probably
know she was back in Ward 3 last week having
made another suicidal attempt.

    Yours sincerely,

    ███████████,
    Physician Superintendent
```

DRUGS & ALCOHOL

GARY MILLAR

DRUGS & ALCOHOL

The next page is simply a brief note in her case file but is probably one of the better hints as to some of Mum's behaviour, albeit it is also one of the saddest.

It mentions screaming - and I remember lots of screaming!

I have learned that, as expected, combining alcohol with, in this case, Tofranil can increase the risk of side effects and adverse reactions. Some of the potential consequences include increased sedation, leading to excessive drowsiness, dizziness, and impaired coordination. Plus, it could also lead to confusion, memory problems, and difficulty in concentrating. It can increase the risk of accidents and injuries, worsen depressive symptoms such as sadness, hopelessness, and suicidal thoughts, cause gastrointestinal upset, affect blood pressure, lead to liver toxicity, and increase the risk of overdose - especially when consuming large amounts of alcohol and Mum enjoyed copious amounts of vodka! She also appeared to suffer many of those side effects throughout all the 60s and 70s.

This note also includes a fleeting comment about an 'attempted abortion.' Separately, and only recently, a 93-year-old relative, then with dementia, and now sadly has died, tells me she remembers Mum telling her she threw herself down a flight of stairs to end a pregnancy. Although not conclusive, that story now makes more sense.

Mon, 19 November 1962

Royal Infirmary Hospital Edinburgh (Outpatient Clinic): Hospital Notes

19.11.62
Back on her Tofranil and feeling rather better.

Father visiting every day.

Is going out drinking when she can get the money and then screams all night.

Feels guilty about the baby and attempted abortion.

PSYCHOPATHIC IMPULSES

GARY MILLAR

PSYCHOPATHIC IMPULSES

This note from 21st November 1962 refers to my Mum's so called 'psychopathic impulses.'

Therefore, I felt obliged to learn more. From my limited or amateur follow-up research it typically refers to urges or desires characteristic of what is called 'psychopathy,' a personality disorder characterised by antisocial behaviour, lack of empathy or remorse, manipulativeness, and a disregard for social norms or laws. People with psychopathy may experience impulses or urges that are harmful to others or violate expected or acceptable normal behaviour, often without the individual feeling guilt or remorse.

When I first read these notes, I was also taken aback by some of the language used to describe both Mum and Dad. Here, within this one, we have such an example 'The general intellectual level is not very high, and she is unable to see very far into the future.' This may be true, but I would argue that although her academic intelligence was most certainly not high, it is a different story when looking at her emotional intelligence. When her mind and body were clear of prescription drugs and alcohol, her emotional intelligence appeared to be exceptional. Unfortunately, there were never too many times when she was clear of both dependencies, so it was always a surprise when she connected with people faster and better than most.

This note also highlights another of her key worries, one that appears to have played continually on her mind for the year following Leslie's birth, and that is her desperation to find a better home. In fact, she spent her later life always looking for a better, more stable place to live!

Wed, 21 November 1962

Bangour Village Hospital: Letter: Letter from Physician Superintendent to GP about Mum's current state of mind

21st November, 1962.

███████,
16, Windsor Street,
EDINBURGH.

Dear ███████,

Mrs. Margaret Millar, 6 East William St., Edinburgh.

I saw Mrs. Millar again on Monday evening and on the previous Monday when she omitted on both occasions to bring with her a letter you had given her for me. As you know, she had a further admission to Ward 3 of the Royal Infirmary on 8th November having taken a few pills during the course of an argument with her husband. She had stopped taking her Tofranil and had consequently been rather more depressed again. When I saw her on Monday, she had again on my instructions gone back on her Tofranil and was feeling rather better. She is, however, in a very unstable state and in addition to her other signs of instability she is going out drinking whenever she can get the money, and then comes home and screams all night. It is very difficult to know what best to do with this young lady. Taking her into hospital would protect her from herself and

SILENT VICTIMS: PART ONE

her psychopathic impulses for a short period and would give her a rest from her family responsibilities. I am quite sure that, as before, she would settle down very quickly in hospital and would very soon lose her symptoms. On the other hand, this would mean that she would promptly discharge herself and would be in the same state as before she came in.

I asked ▉▉▉▉▉▉▉ to visit her with regard to her housing problem, and he tells me that he has given her some extra points which may help her to get another house in the not-too-distant future. I had also thought a Health Visitor might look in and help her with the problem of looking after the family, but this does not seem to have been followed up by the Public Health Department. I think that on the whole it might be better if one of our own Social Workers could look in and give her some support. She feels very guilty about her disabled baby as is common with mothers of disabled children, and this is part responsible for her feelings of depression and aggression towards her husband. The general intellectual level is not very high, and she is unable to see very far into the future. I think it might be useful to add 10 mgms of Librium t.i.d. to her Tofranil.

Yours sincerely,
▉▉▉▉▉▉▉,
Physician Superintendent

Mon, 26 November 1962

Royal Infirmary Hospital Edinburgh (Outpatient Clinic): Hospital Notes

```
   26.11.62
```
Not sleeping too well, but otherwise not too bad.

Nowhere ready to go if she got out alone.

Baby is fine, but still has a cough. Has not seen ████████ since last visit.

Children not at nursery just now.

SILENT VICTIMS: PART ONE

Wed, 28 November 1962

Social Worker: Report by Mum's first Social Worker

28.11.62
Home visit. Two friends and children were in. Mrs. Millar talked of how depressed she got with her small house, and how she snaps at anyone who 'said a wrong word.' She says she was always sorry to snap at the children, as they were just babies. The two elder children are not attending the nursery just now, as they have not been well. She spoke of the baby and says he was a 'wee doll' and that she gave him too much attention, to make up to him for his deformity.

After her neighbour and friend had gone, she expressed irritation that the neighbour, with her children, came down to her house too often. She said she had no one to baby-sit for her so that she could get out with her husband, and that this neighbour had not offered. She will not go out by herself, although her husband is good at housekeeping and is willing to stay in to let her have an evening out.

Mrs. Millar produced the baby for my inspection and let me hold him for a while. She talks to him although she does not know if he can hear her. She showed me his hearing aid and told me he cannot keep it on his head, she wondered if 2 head bands would help.

I suggested that I could visit her at intervals, to see how she was managing, and she seemed pleased at this, as she says she very seldom sees anyone but her neighbour.

The Sanitary Inspector has called, and says she is not overcrowded until the baby is one year old.

GARY MILLAR

4.12.62

Mrs. Millar was pleased to have a visitor. She had been alone all day, as her neighbour's husband has left her, and the neighbour has been expecting her mother-in-law to come. Mrs. Millar had not wanted to intrude but talked about the situation with interest. She felt the neighbour was in as much need of psychiatric help as she had been, and wondered if she ought to tell a doctor. I suggested that her first concern should be her own health, and that of her family, as she was not really fit to have more worries.

The middle son, Norman, has measles, so none of the children are at the nursery.

Mrs. Millar seemed fairly bright, but says she is still up and down a lot.

Her neighbour came in later, and I left shortly after this, as it was clearly impracticable, in the circumstances, to carry on a conversation about Mrs. Millar's problems.

I am to visit next week.

SILENT VICTIMS: PART ONE

Mon, 10 December 1962

Royal Infirmary Hospital Edinburgh (Outpatient Clinic): Hospital Notes

```
10.12.62
```
Wee one has a lot of diarrhoea. Next one has measles.
    Feeling tired with nursing etc.
    Got tablets from ███████.
    ███████ (**Author's edit:** Mum's longest serving Social Worker) is a support to her.
    Church people have been to see her too.
    Stomach was upset on Saturday and not right since.
    Not eating well but is putting on weight.

Thu, 20 December 1962

Social Worker: Report by Mum's first Social Worker

20.12.62
Mrs. Millar was looking very white and had been feeling unwell all day. She had been so depressed that she had felt quite unable to cope with the children, and her neighbours had taken them off her hands for a while in the morning. Both elder boys have had measles, but the baby, Leslie, has not. We tried Leslie's hearing aid on his head and I held him while Mrs. Millar and her neighbour tried to attract his attention by snapping fingers, playing a musical teddy bear, etc. Mrs. Millar keeps this toy, which looked expensive, exclusively for Leslie, and will not allow the other children to touch it. She appears to be adjusting to Leslie's deformity.

Mrs. Millar has been disappointed by the housing department who have said that she will not be eligible for a new house until her elder son, who is now three years old, is 10 years old. The thought of another 7 years in East William Street, depresses her.

We talked of the possibility of her coming to the Wednesday Club, and I suggested that she talk it over with her husband. She seemed fairly keen on the idea, and we agreed to discuss it again in the New Year.

HOGMANAY 1962

GARY MILLAR

HOGMANAY 1962

Mum loved Hogmanay. It was one of her annual highlights and is still one of Scotland's most important celebrations. Festivities often lasted for days and gave an opportunity for friends and family to come together and celebrate the beginning of a new year. In fact, Mum often dreamt of the new beginnings each new year would bring. One full of promise and hopefully with no more demons. She would often talk about the first footer bringing a lump of coal for the fire and a drink or two to celebrate the year about to begin.

As we waited for the midnight bells, we watched 'The King of Hogmanay' Andy Stewart on our black-and-white TV. To the swirl of kilts and the sound of bagpipes and accordions, the likes of The White Heather Dancers, Duncan Macrae, Jimmy Logan, Jimmy Shand and his band also entertained us. Counting down to midnight, we laughed and loved Andy's hit Donald Where's Yer Troosers and teared up to his A Scottish Soldier.

Adult Hogmanay also meant advocaat and fizzy lemonade Snowball cocktails, cheese, and pineapple on cocktail sticks, washed down with copious glasses of Babysham, vodka or whisky. As children, our Hogmanay parties give us our first taste of a thimble of Snowball, Christmas leftover marzipan fruits and maraschino cherries, I suppose destined for the adult's cocktails.

Yes, Hogmanay was Mum's big reset button, but it changed little in our lives. In fact, it often made her screams a lot louder, and once the festivities had ended, her clouds of depression were a lot darker!

GARY MILLAR

31.12.62

Home visit. Both Mr. and Mrs. Millar at home. Mr. Millar had been off work for a few days with a slight illness. He is a slightly built, fair-haired man, of medium height, and looks several years younger than his wife. He has a high-pitched voice and talks in a rather immature way.

They were preparing for Hogmanay visitors, and Mrs. Millar, although she had washed her hair for the occasion, did not seem to be looking forward to it. Her husband said he was determined not to let her drink too much, and to make her eat something before she had anything to drink, as she had been off her food for several days. Mrs. Millar felt she would like to make herself drunk, and we all discussed this, her husband and I dissuading her.

The relationship between them seemed fairly good, and Mr. Millar seemed fairly competent to help with the children. He brought Leslie through for me to see. We talked of Mrs. Millar's coming to the Wednesday Club and both seemed fairly enthusiastic. This is to be arranged.

Author's Notes:

An interesting description of my father in the first paragraph above. One that at once brought back vivid memories of hearing his voice.

Mum and Dad at Wilkie House

WILKIE HOUSE

WILKIE HOUSE WEDNESDAY CLUB

Following Leslie's birth, Mum's surrogate place of worship was her Wednesday visits to Wilkie House Cabaret Club. Ironically, a former church, at 207 Cowgate, Edinburgh. About 550 yards southeast of Edinburgh Castle, and part of the lower level of Edinburgh's Old Town, below the elevated streets of South Bridge and George IV Bridge. Wilkie House briefly reopened as Faith, before it became Stamash.

It's seen its fair share of dance enthusiasts over the years! Mum loved this place and often returned on Saturdays to drink and, of course, to dance.

4.1.63

Short visit to see that Mrs. Millar survived New Year's celebrations. She seemed alright. Next week's meeting of the Wednesday Club is to be a committee meeting, so will take her to the next one – she is agreeable to this.

14.1.63

Mrs. Millar had set the chimney on fire several days ago, so the room was heated by an oil heater, as the chimney was damaged. She had taken this accident very calmly and told me it had not upset her.

The children were back to the nursery, so she has less to cope with during the day. Mr. Millar is back to work. Mrs. Millar's appointment with ▇▇▇▇▇▇ was not kept, because she had had the children at home and no baby-sitter. She was anxious to have another appointment.

Mrs. Millar was less anxious and depressed than she has been. She's going to a dance soon, and she had bought a new dress with which she was very pleased. We arranged that she should come to the Wilkie House Club a week on Wednesday. I am to collect her.

Leslie was brought through when I asked about him. He is reaching out for things now, and grasps objects held out to him. He has to go back to hospital to have his hearing aid adjusted.

Mrs. Millar seemed, on the whole to be keeping better this week.

SILENT VICTIMS: PART ONE

Tue, 22 January 1963

Social Worker: Letter to Mum about attending the Wilkie House Wednesday Club

22nd January, 1963.

Mrs. Marjorie Millar,
6, East William Street,
EDINBURGH.

Dear Mrs. Millar,

I called to see you last night and was sorry that you were out. However, I should like to come to collect you on Wednesday evening at 7 o'clock, as we arranged, and to go to Wilkie House Wednesday Club with you. The programme for the evening will include a cabaret show, which should be amusing.

I look forward to seeing you then.

Yours sincerely,

███████████,
Social Worker.

GARY MILLAR

Wed, 23 January 1963

Social Worker: Report by Mum's first Social Worker

23.1.63
Called to collect Mrs. Millar to go to the Wednesday Club and was informed by her husband that she had gastritis and was in bed. She had been taken to The Royal Infirmary on Friday by emergency ambulance, as her husband had been worried in case she had an ulcer. He has one himself, so was probably made nervous by the appearance of similar symptoms in his wife. Mr. Millar was coping with the two elder boys, and Leslie was in his pram in the same room as his mother. He smiles quite frequently now, and has a fairly strong grip, and reacts to attempts to play with him.

Mrs. Millar was feeling better than she had been, but still weak. She had had solid food that day and had not been sick. She was miserable, but not as depressed as might have been expected.

Am to visit on Monday.

28.1.63
Mrs. Millar was very depressed, began to tell me everything that was wrong, and burst into tears. Her stomach is still very upset, she has flatulence and fears that something more serious than gastritis is wrong, her greatest fear for herself being that she has cancer. She has recently discovered that Leslie has something wrong with his spine. ('it stops, then curves away'). Asked her to bring him through to show me, and she did. There was some curving of the

spine, but there was not a gap in the middle as she had thought. She was comparing his growth with that of other younger babies who could sit up while Leslie couldn't, and anxious about his failure to put on weight. Her next appointment at the hospital is in March. I held him for a while and we discussed him, and Mrs. Millar began to tell me about her pain and discomfort while she was carrying him, and her resentment at the fact that she was not told that there was anything wrong with the baby. From there, she went on to tell about her fears of becoming pregnant again and said she had been given the address of a Family Planning Clinic by the doctor, but that she could not afford to go, as she thought the first visit cost £1, and she had been afraid to tell the doctor this. I said I would find out about this for her. She was worried about not being able to use her appliance properly, and I assured her that she would be taught. Her doctor had already told her this, but she is still apprehensive.

Mr. Millar brought the children home from the nursery. He rebuked Mrs. Millar for not having been to her doctor about her stomach and she began to cry again. The two elder children are very sympathetic when she cries and ask if she is not well. Mr. Millar was very good with her too. He does a lot of the housework. Neither of them is keen now to go to the dance they had planned to attend; suggested it would help them.

Am to go back on Wednesday.

30.1.63
Phoned ▇▇▇▇ of Family Planning Association and procured details of clinics and payments and arranged to take Mrs. Millar to a clinic next Tuesday afternoon.

Home visit to Mrs. Millar. She was still

depressed, but not quite so anxious as on Monday. She had been unable to get up in the morning early enough to take the children to the nursery, so had had them all day. She and her husband had again examined Leslie's spine and compared it with Gary's and have decided that it is no different from his; Mrs. Millar was relieved at this.

Mr. Millar came in. We all discussed Mrs. Millar's health and his and eventually the Family Planning Clinic. Told Mrs. Millar we would be able to help her financially to buy contraceptive appliances and asked them about their finances with a view to getting exemption from paying doctors' fees. A Tuesday afternoon visit will be convenient for her.

Gave Mrs. Millar appointment to see ▮▮▮▮▮▮▮ on Monday at 5 p.m.

SILENT VICTIMS: PART ONE

Mon, 4 February 1963

Royal Infirmary Hospital Edinburgh (Outpatient Clinic): Hospital Notes

```
4.2.63
```
Not been keeping well at all. Feeling depressed, not eating. Feels she can't do her work, can't get out, can't cope with the children.
　Doesn't want to go out, goes about like a tramp in the house.
　Stomach not bothering her too much.
　Her own family upset her, tell her she is 'off her head,' so she doesn't visit.
　Mother-in-law is better to her but can't manage out. Feeling 'awfy' tired.

FAMILY PLANNING

GARY MILLAR

FAMILY PLANNING

It would appear from a couple of comments in this case file that Mum was extremely worried about becoming pregnant again. Fortunately, her Social Worker made efforts to help Mum visit the Mothers' Welfare Clinic and manage her contraceptive prescription.

Mrs. Hazel Kennedy established the Edinburgh Mothers' Welfare Clinic, as it was first known in 1933, to 'give instruction in the most satisfactory methods of contraception to married women in poor circumstances.'

In response to increasing demand, the clinic moved into 18 Dean Terrace in 1957. Lothian Health Board took over the service in 1974 as part of the reorganisation of the National Health Service. They later changed the name to the Edinburgh Family Planning Trust in 1988.

Although not discussed in her case file, Mum did not become pregnant again. However, it later becomes clear that she developed a strong wish to have just one more baby.

This note also mentions a neighbour's overdose and Mum's ability to manage this situation.

In addition, the following pages repeat an often-discussed issue in these notes where Norman and I often could not attend nursery because Mum could not get up in time to take us.

Tue, 5 February 1963

Social Worker: Report by Mum's first Social Worker

5.2.63
Went with Mrs. Millar to Mothers' Welfare Clinic, 18 Dean Terrace. It was found that a contraceptive cap would be unsuitable for her, and that she should be given oral contraceptives. Her GPs permission had to be obtained, so an appointment was made for her to go back to the clinic tomorrow, with a note giving his written permission.

6.2.63
Phoned ▇▇▇▇▇ of F.P.A. (**Author's edit:** Family Planning) I was told that Mrs. Millar visit had been satisfactory. ▇▇▇▇▇ explained how Mrs. Millar's contraceptive pills should be taken and has asked me to help her if necessary. A further appointment has been made for her, and I am to accompany her.

14.2.63
Mrs. Millar's neighbour was in, having taken an overdose of tablets containing phenobarbitone. She had been sick twice and Mrs. Millar had phoned her doctor and had been told how to look after her and was doing this. All 4 older children were there. Mrs. Millar seemed capable of handling the situation and dwelt for a while on her neighbour's problems before reverting to her own.

She has received her first lot of contraceptive pills, and was worried because she

SILENT VICTIMS: PART ONE

had been given 100, instead of 20, as she had been led to expect. We decided it would relieve her mind if we counted out 20, which she put in an envelope and locked in her medicine box, and I took away the rest.

Mrs. Millar had not been able to get up in time to take the children to nursery most mornings. She says she is neglecting them. We agreed that I might visit her early in the morning one day to see if she has been able to get up and go to the nursery, this might give her some incentive.

I asked for Leslie, and she brought him through. His feet were very cold, and Mrs. Millar says he will not keep socks on. We discussed methods of keeping him warm.

Mrs. Millar's physical health is better than it has been recently. She is eating better and sleeps fairly well.

18.2.63

Visited about 9 a.m. Mrs. Millar had just awakened the children and hadn't been able to wake up in time to go to the nursery.

She had had a fairly peaceful weekend, and no further crisis with her neighbour.

I took her pills with me, and together, we counted them into 20s, and put them into numbered envelopes, so that she will not become muddled about how many she has used. She has not begun using them yet.

Mon, 18 February 1963

Edinburgh Corporation: Letter of reply from Social Worker to Medical Officer of Health about re-housing

███████████,
Medical Officer of Health,
Edinburgh Corporation Public Health Department,
Johnston Terrace,
EDINBURGH, 1

Dear ███████████,

Mrs. Margaret Millar, 6, East William Street, Edinburgh.

I have been working with Mrs. Millar, who is an out-patient at ███████████'s clinic at Sighthill and understand that ███████████ has mentioned her case to you, and the question of her housing conditions. Mrs. Millar tells me that, on the last occasion, when she enquired about her prospects of housing, she was told that she would have to wait until her eldest son, who is now 3 years old, is 10 years old, before she is considered to be overcrowded. Can you tell me if this is correct, please, and if it is whether there is anything more you can do to forward Mrs. Millar's case? It is felt that it would be most advantageous to her mental and physical health, to have some more immediate prospect of adequate housing arrangements.

Yours sincerely,
███████████,
Social Worker.

SILENT VICTIMS: PART ONE

Thu, 21 February 1963

Social Worker: Report by Mum's first Social Worker

```
21.2.63
```
Mrs. Millar was looking brighter than she had been. Her period of menstruation had started, and she had begun filling in her chart. This is the first day, so I am to visit again on Tuesday, when she will have taken her first contraceptive pill. She had no worries about it.

Mr. Millar and both older boys were there. Mrs. Millar has not been able to take the children to the nursery all week.

The district nurse has called, and Mrs. Millar has spoken to her about her anxiety concerning Leslie.

After having seen the photograph in a newspaper of people at the Wednesday Club Dance, Mrs. Millar is most enthusiastic to go, and asked me to collect her next week. She mentioned this of her own accord.

GARY MILLAR

Fri, 22 February 1963

Bangour Village Hospital: Reply from Edinburgh Corporation to Social Worker about 'housing points'

```
                            Edinburgh Corporation
                         Public Health Department
                                Johnston Terrace,
                                     Edinburgh 1

                            22nd February, 1963.

                                ███████████,
                                   Social Worker,
                         Bangour Village Hospital,
                                        BROXBURN,
                                    West Lothian.
```

Dear ███████,

Re: Mrs. Margaret Millar, 6 East William St.

Thank you for your letter about this patient. I know this case well and feel extremely sorry for Mrs. Millar. It is true that the house has not been considered to be overcrowded but because of my concern for the case, I took the matter up with the Housing people and did award 4 medical points. I don't think there is much more I can do but I will be seeing the Housing Officer again fairly soon. I will bring Mrs. Millar's case up.

Yours sincerely,
███████████
Medical Officer for Mental Health Services.

Mum with Leslie, Gary, and Norman (1963)

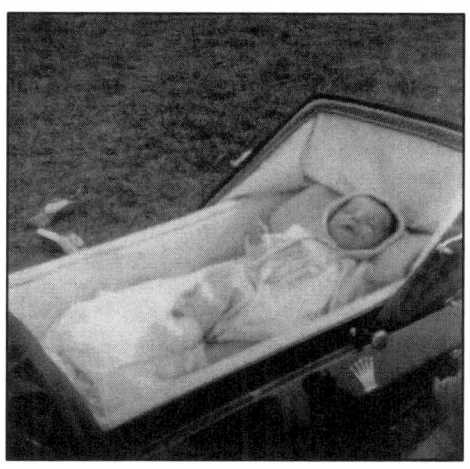

Leslie in a pram (1963)

LESLIE'S FIRST PHOTOGRAPHS

LESLIE'S FIRST PHOTOGRAPH

This social worker's note mentions Leslie's photograph being taken by, I am assuming, a professional photographer. Coincidentally, I had come across this same photo for the first time in January 2022. I had also found another, obviously taken at the same time. This second photo includes me, Leslie, on Dad's lap, Dad, and our brother Norman. It is obvious, looking at these photos, that Mum is correct in thinking that the photo could have been better, as in both, everyone, except Dad, is looking elsewhere.

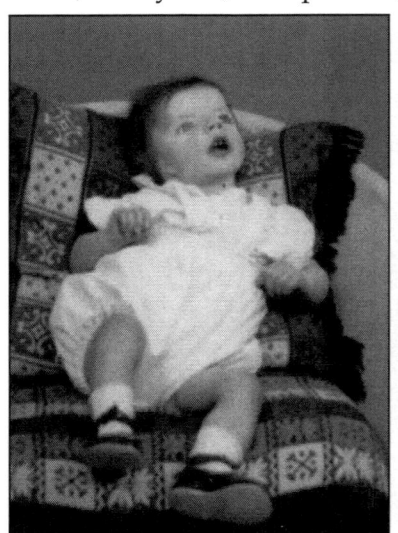

I find the next note, together with the photos above, emotional. Particularly when I have now been able to bring together 2 previously unrelated details! Mum appears to be talking to us through time by referencing at least one of these photographs – and from over 60 years ago!

GARY MILLAR

Tue, 26 February 1963

Social Worker: Report by Mum's first Social Worker

26.2.63

Spoke to ▮▮▮▮▮▮▮▮, health visitor for Mrs. Millar's area, as Mrs. Millar had mentioned me to her. She felt that Mrs. Millar was rejecting Leslie, as he is never in the living room with the rest of the family when she calls. She told me, when I asked, how she thought he ought to be fed, and has told Mrs. Millar this, too. She is unable to get an answer always when she calls and is often unable to see Mrs. Millar when she is upstairs at her neighbour's.

27.2.63

Mr. Millar was at home on holiday and was doing the household washing in the washing machine. Norman was at home, as he had a cold, but Gary had been taken to the nursery by his father. Leslie was in bed – he had been in the living room but had been washed and was now in the bedroom.

Mrs. Millar had taken her first contraceptive pill last night (Tuesday, 26 February), and had felt faintly sick and headachy, but had been told to expect this and was accepting it. She had Leslie's photograph taken, and was fairly pleased with it, but felt it could have been better. Had the man had more patience with the child, and waited until he was still. I took a copy of the photograph to show ▮▮▮▮▮▮▮▮.

Told Mrs. Millar that I had spoken to ▮▮▮▮▮▮▮▮, her health visitor, and that ▮▮▮▮▮▮▮▮ had replied to my letter about her

SILENT VICTIMS: PART ONE

re-housing. We made arrangements for her visit to the Wednesday Club.

Discuss the idea of Leslie going to a special school, and the prospect of having to look after a handicapped child for years. Was shown his hearing aid with its new headband and discussed feeding Leslie. Mrs. Millar was apprehensive about the reactions of other children to Leslie when he was old enough to mix with them. Discussed his hearing aid and am to help with his training session with it next time I go.

7.3.63

Upstairs neighbour, plus her two children were in. Mrs. Millar's two eldest were at home, as they have colds. Leslie was in the other room.

While ███████ was there Mrs. Millar told me that she had been very depressed and that she had wanted to come back into hospital on Friday night. She had been screaming and had thrown the key of her wooden 'pillbox' at her husband, and also the box. This box has been gaily decorated and is receiving an undue amount of attention. The children have been warned not to touch it, but are, naturally, very curious about it.

Mrs. Millar came to the Wednesday Club on 27th February, and I saw her to her bus afterwards. When she had arrived home, she had felt like jumping up and down in the middle of the floor and putting her hand through the window. Her husband has been coming home drunk fairly often recently, and refuses to help with the housework at present, and had punished the eldest child severely last night.

Author's Note:

One of the earliest indications of Dad's anger issues and his violence towards his children, in this case, me!

```
    When  ████████████  had gone, Mrs. Millar told
me that she had kept the children at home really
because she was frightened on her own. She has
begun to hear voices and is afraid she is going
mad. She had wanted very badly to come into
hospital on Friday.
    I question her about the voices and was told
they were neither men's nor women's voices, but
like 'wee elves,' all trying to crowd out her
thoughts. She does not know what they are
saying, but feels they are trying to take over
her mind. She has told no one about them.
```

Author's Note:
In later years, I have clear memories of Mum explaining to me she often heard voices!

She talked a lot about her husband and married life and about occasions on which she felt he had been unfaithful to her.

Author's Note:
Through her drunken screams and tears, Mum continued to question Dad's infidelities for the next 40 years.

```
    17.3.63
    Home visit at 9:20 a.m. Mrs. Millar was just
getting the children out of bed, and dress them
while we were talking. The two children were
looking well and seemed happy to be home. Gary,
the elder, says he does not want to go back to
school. Norman is apparently happy but is
wetting during the day, Mrs. Millar says.
```

SILENT VICTIMS: PART ONE

Gary explained to me that Leslie is staying in the nursery. Mrs. Millar said that she had had a look at him before she took them home, but that her husband only had visited him yesterday so that she would not be upset.

Author's Note:
I remember none of the above.

Mrs. Millar was very quiet – this may have been because she does not awaken readily in the morning. She says she is sleeping but not eating much. Her visit to the Family Planning Clinic has been uneventful – she had felt quite confident – but she is to go back in two weeks' time to have her change of pills checked upon. She had mentioned the matter of sterilisation to one of the doctors there who had agreed to look into the matter.

Mrs. Millar says that the children were 'a pair of menaces,' and will not do what they are told, but that she was pleased she had brought them home.

Arranged a visit in a few days' time, as she was so listless.

SUICIDE RISK

SUICIDE RISK

Although there appears to be no admission records in Mum's case file attributed to this episode, it is clear from the notes that Mum entered Ward 3, Royal Infirmary Hospital on the Friday morning, of 29th March 1963, as a grave suicide risk.

This was coincidentally on the same day as the fifth anniversary of her marriage.

Following a trip to Wilkie House, she had swallowed about fifteen tablets on that same Wednesday evening and had called her GP on the Thursday seeking help. He had therefore requested her admission to Bangour Village Hospital.

Eventually, they admitted her to Ward 2, Bangour Village Hospital on Friday, 12th April 1963. Therefore, I assume she remained in the Royal throughout the period leading up to that admission.

I also know from my separate Scottish Social Services Council (SSSC) records that after my dad applied to have Norman and me taken into care, they admitted us to St Helen's Nursery Children's Home on 2nd April, 1963.

My SSSC records also noted that 'she will be in for approximately 3 months and that there were no relatives available.'

SILENT VICTIMS: PART ONE

The hospital eventually discharged Mum from Bangour Village Hospital on 22nd May, 1963. Although Norman and I remained under care until 3 weeks later, until Friday, 14th June 1963.

GARY MILLAR

Mon, 1 April 1963

Social Worker: Report by Mum's first Social Worker

1.4.63

███████████, Almoner, R.I.E. telephoned to say that Mrs. Marjorie Millar requested her to inform you that she is in hospital. ███████ has spoken to ███████████ (**Author's Edit**: Physician Superintendent) about Mrs. Millar's transfer here but has so far heard no more about this as ███████████ was going to investigate the bed position here and let ███████████ know. Could you please telephone ███████████ tomorrow morning, TUESDAY, after 9.30 a.m. at Ward 3, R.I.E?

1.4.63

Was informed by ███████████ (**Author's Edit**: Physician Superintendent) that Mrs. Millar was admitted to Ward 3, Royal Infirmary, early on Friday morning, as a grave suicide risk. She had been sent there by her GP, who was called on Thursday night and is now awaiting admission to Bangour.

Phoned Ward 3 and contacted ███████████, P.S.W., to find out what had happened to the children. He said ███████████, GP, appeared to have made necessary arrangements. Mrs. Millar had, evidently, swallowed a number of tablets on Wednesday night, but had said she did not remember doing this, but had wakened up with the bottle of pills in her hand. ███████████ said Mrs. Millar had told him that she had been to Wilkie House Club on Wednesday, but that, unfortunately, the social work staff from

SILENT VICTIMS: PART ONE

Bangour had been on holiday. ▆▆▆▆▆▆▆ told me that Mr. Millar, and the children had been in to see her on Sunday (her wedding anniversary) and had brought her flowers.

I asked if I might go to Ward 3 to see to see Mrs. Millar, and ▆▆▆▆▆▆▆ offered to arrange this with Sister, and to ask that I be shown Mrs. Millar's case notes.

Interview with Mrs. Millar. She looked dazed and was in a hospital dressing gown but wearing a pair of new slippers. She told me that she was feeling very weepy, most of the time, and that she had been getting worse for several days before Wednesday, when she had without knowing it swallowed about 15 tablets. This had frightened her, and she had asked her husband to phone her GP, who when he had seen her, had taken her into the Royal 'in case anything happened.' She had been feeling like going away and taking a room on her own, leaving the children and her husband. Then she had felt she must get back into hospital and is anxious to stay until she gets better, this time – 'for the sake of the kids and my husband.' Mrs. Millar says that she was worried about the children; she wondered if Leslie would be taking into a home since he is disabled, was distressed by the fact that Gary was in tears on Sunday, and that he understands that he has to go to another home while his mother is in hospital. Norman had been quiet, and she felt he was not well. Leslie had boils on his head again.

We discussed the possibility of Leslie's staying in care because of his handicap, but Mrs. Millar says she is not keen about this, and would have to have him at home, at least at weekends.

She is worried by bills which have not been paid and said that this week's financial arrangements would be put out as she had had new slippers bought for her. Suggested that I might call on Mr. Millar to give him some help with straightening things out before she went home, and she was pleased about this. She is worried that he may start drinking heavily, as he has done before, and that he might be unfaithful to her.

We arranged that she should ask him if he would like me to visit, and that I should see her on Wednesday.

3.4.63

Mrs. Millar was in bed. She was still looking dazed, but in course of conversation said that she was beginning to take an interest in things again, e.g. had put her hair in rollers.

She said early in the conversation that she had been thinking a lot about Leslie and did not want to give him up. She had told ▇▇▇▇▇▇▇ who had told her not to worry about this till he was better, and I reassured her that nothing would be done until she was ready for it and able to make up her own mind.

The conversation was largely about the children, as on Monday, and Mrs. Millar was worried about having Leslie taken to his appointment at the Sick Children's Hospital on Friday. ▇▇▇▇▇▇▇, P.S.W. has been arranging this; said I would see her.

Interview with ▇▇▇▇▇▇▇; she is having Leslie taken to the Sick Children's, but I am to carry on work with rest of family.

4.4.63

Interview with Mr. Millar at home. He will be, I think, unwilling to accept help with his financial muddle, though he admits that things

SILENT VICTIMS: PART ONE

are in a mess. He was inclined to blame his wife for this, saying that she had not kept up payments. E.g. for foster parents (she had blamed this on him) and said he was too soft with her and let her have too much. He had a letter from the Children's Department about charges for the care of the children and arrears; agreed to contact the Department to ask about reducing this, but we agreed that he should contact them too.

We talked about plans for Leslie's future, and he says he wants to keep him, and went on to talk of his birth, and his feelings on being told about him, and of how he had to cope with Mrs. Millar's feelings of grief and resentment.

We arranged that I should make further arrangements to see him when I next saw Mrs. Millar.

GARY MILLAR

Thu, 4 April 1963

Bangour Village Hospital: Letter from Psychiatric Social Worker to Social Worker about testing Leslie

```
THE ROYAL INFIRMARY OF EDINBURGH
DEPARTMENT OF PSYCHOLOGICAL MEDICINE
                      East Medical Block
             Royal Infirmary, Edinburgh.
```

4th April 1963

Dear ███████,

A further development in Mrs. Millar's case - I spoke again to , Almoner, Sick Children's Hospital who confirmed that Leslie will be kept in hospital on Friday so that they can test him thoroughly. I'll tell Mrs. Millar about this and arrange to ring ███████ on Wednesday next week to get a report about Leslie of by this time Mrs. Millar has left Ward 3, I'll let you know what the report is. It was nice to have met you yesterday and good of you to come up. Hope to see you again soon.

Sincerely,

,
P.S.W.

SILENT VICTIMS: PART ONE

Fri, 12 April 1963

Bangour Village Hospital (Ward 2): Admission Notes - includes possessions list, height, height, temperature, pulse and respn

```
12.4.63
IN POSSESSION ON ADMISSION

1 Coat
1 Dress
2 Skirts
3 Cardigans
3 Jumpers
2 Bras
3 Underskirts
5 Pr pants
5 Nightdresses
1 Suspender Belt
1 Pr Slippers
1 Pr Shoes
1 Bed Jacket
1 Dressing gown
Wedding ring with patient
Purse containing £1-5-11 1/2 with patient

Height: 5ft 5"
Weight: 10st 2 1/2
Temp: 97
Pulse: 84
Respn: 20
```

Author's Notes:
Date of admission: 12.04.63 at 10:30am Date of discharge: 22.05.63.

Fri, 12 April 1963

Bangour Village Hospital: Admission from 12.04.63 - 22.05.1963

12.4.63
Date of Admission: 12.4.63
Admitted from home, quiet and cooperative since admission.

13.4.63
Emotional in forenoon, to have Tryptizol 50 mg T.I.D.

15.4.63
Very disturbed and anxious about her baby in AM. More settled after seeing social worker. Tryptizol discontinued. Melleril increased to 75 mgs T.I.D.
Chest x-ray this forenoon.

20.4.63
Vomited undigested food at 4 PM.

Sat, 20 April 1963

Bangour General Hospital: X-ray result

```
MILLAR Marjorie Ward 2
Chest - Negative

Signature          ▇▇▇▇▇▇.
```

SILENT VICTIMS: PART ONE

Sun, 21 April 1963

Bangour Village Hospital: Patient's Notes

21.4.63
Confirmation of nausea this afternoon, vomit green when going to toilet and felt dizzy, put back to bed T.P.R. 98 90/20. Medical officer notified. Patient appears much better tonight.

22.4.63
Good day, no further sickness.

23.4.63
Distressed in forenoon. More settled and happier in afternoon and evening. To continue Melleril 75 mgs T.I.D.

25.4.63
Continues to improve. Up this afternoon. To rest in bed forenoon, no further sickness. Taking full diet.

Fri, 26 April 1963

Social Worker: Report by Mum's first Social Worker

26.4.63

Interview with Mrs. Millar. Have seen her almost every day and her attitude towards Leslie's future has been ambivalent and confused. She has introduced the subject voluntarily on almost all occasions; I have not persuaded either to keep him or to put him into residential care for handicapped children, but have explained, what possibilities are there are.

Today she says she has decided to 'give Leslie up' for a year or two to see how he will develop with specialised care. She feels it would be to his own advantage to do this.

SILENT VICTIMS: PART ONE

Fri, 26 April 1963

Social Worker: Letter from Social Worker to Dad about Financial Commitments

```
                              26th April, 1963.

                            Mr. Gordon Millar,
                         6, East William Street,
                                      Edinburgh.
```

Dear Mr. Millar,

I have asked Mrs. Millar to discuss with you the question of my seeing the Children's Officer in connection with your payments to St. Helens. This will, as I have mentioned, involve my giving to Mr. Millar, Children's Officer, a detailed account of your financial affairs, including all your commitments. If you are agreeable to my doing this, I should like to come down on Monday, 29th April, about 5 p.m. to gather the information from you. Could you please tell Mrs. Millar on Saturday if this would be convenient?

Yours sincerely,

,
Social Worker.

GARY MILLAR

Fri, 26 April 1963

Bangour Village Hospital: Letter from Registrar to Bangour General Hospital

26th April, 1963.

███████████,
Bangour General Hospital,
Broxburn.

Dear ███████████,

Mrs Margaret Millar - Ward 2.

I would be glad if you would give me an appointment for this woman, who complains of foul-smelling vaginal discharge. She has a fairly severe degree of hypochromic anaemia but does not admit to any menorrhagia.

Yours sincerely,

███████████,
Registrar.

Sat, 27 April 1963

Bangour Village Hospital: Patient's Notes

27.4.63

```
Both breasts hard and tender. Left breast badly
swollen. Crepe bandages applied for support.
Resting in bed today.
```

DAD'S MESSAGE FROM THE PAST

GARY MILLAR

DAD'S MESSAGE FROM THE PAST

Until receiving Mum's case file, I did not have any examples of letters or notes written by him. This was another emotional discovery amongst Mum's Case File.

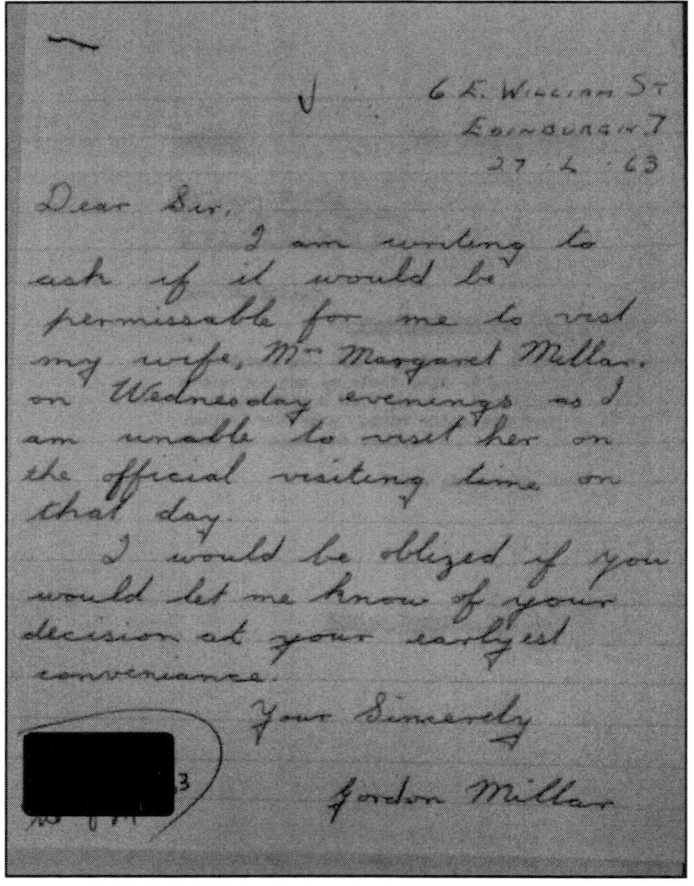

SILENT VICTIMS: PART ONE

Sat, 27 April 1963

Dad: Handwritten request to Bangour Village Hospital requesting to visit Mum on Wednesday evenings

6 East William St
Edinburgh 7
Scotland

Dear Sir,

I am writing to ask if it would be permissible for me to visit my wife, Mrs Margaret Millar, on Wednesday evenings as I am unable to visit her on the official visiting time on that day.

I would be obliged if you would let me know of your decision at your earliest convenience.

Yours sincerely,

Gordon Millar

███████████. Notified 29/4/63

Sun, 28 April 1963

Bangour Village Hospital: Patient's Notes

28.4.63
Breast less painful, remained in bed.

29.4.63
Breast less painful and swollen today. Both breasts secreting milk.

SILENT VICTIMS: PART ONE

Mon, 29 April 1963

Social Worker: Report by Mum's first Social Worker

29.4.63
Mrs. Millar cheerful though troubled by very sore breasts. Her physical condition seems very poor, but she seems to be seeing this as rather a joke at the moment – 'I have something different every day.'

Including Social Worker's interview with Dad and breakdown of monthly expenditure

29.4.63
Interviewed Mr. Millar at home. He had written out a fairly comprehensive report of his financial commitments – which amount to within £4 to £10 of his whole monthly wage. He agreed that the situation was grave and said many payments were in arrears. He has written to several firms to try to avoid court action. Warned him of the expense involved in court proceedings.

I offered to, and he was quite willing that I should, see the Children's Officer to try to have payments for the children made less.

He is prepared to send back his rented TV set, as he reads and does not need it. As it was bought for Mrs. Millar will see how she feels about this.

Discussed Leslie's future. Mr. Millar said that if Mrs. Millar wish to have him taken him into care, he was quite agreeable, as he felt that she had had enough to cope with, with the rest of the family.

He is anxious to visit in the evening during the week.

```
MRS MGT MILLAR - LIST OF MONTHLY EXPENDITURE
DRAWN UP BY Mr. Millar
   MARCH '63 (PER MONTH)
   MAITLAND ELECTRIC: £1.0.10d
   MAITLAND RADIO: £3.4.4
   PETER ALLANS CLOTHES: £3.8
   SLOANS CLOTHES & HOUSEHOLD: £5
   RICHIE CLOTHES: £12
   MASON ELECTRIC: £2
   WAVERLEY BOOK COMPANY: £1.10
   RENT OF HOUSE: £2.17.10
   ELECTRICITY: £2 AVERAGE
   INSURANCE (UNITED FRIENDLY): £1.6.8
   COAL: £2
   NATIONAL INSURANCE: £2.2.4

   TOTAL EXPENDITURE
   £39.10

   MONTHLY WAGE
   £10.80 PER WEEK = £41.12 PER MONTH

   DIFFERENCE
   £2.0.2
```

Author's Note:

It is obvious from the above that with a difference of only £2 between total fixed expenditure and Dad's monthly wage, there was little room for buying food, travel expenses, maintenance payments and incidentals – like the new slippers mentioned previously on 01.04.63.

SILENT VICTIMS: PART ONE

Mon, 29 April 1963

Bangour Village Hospital: Letter from Senior Hospital Medical Officer to Dad agreeing visits on Wednesday evenings to see Mum

```
                                    29th April, 1963.

                                    Mr. Gordon Millar,
                              6 East William Street,
                                       Edinburgh, 7.

Dear Mr. Millar,

Mrs Margaret Millar, Ward 2.
   Thank you for your letter. It will be in order
for you to visit your wife on Wednesday evenings
from 6 to 7 p.m. I enclose a special visiting
permit which you should bring with you when you
visit.

   Yours sincerely,

   ▆▆▆▆▆▆▆▆,
   Senior Hospital Medical Officer.
```

Wed, 1 May 1963

Bangour Village Hospital: Patient's Notes

1.5.63
Seen by ███████, prescribed treatment continues.

SILENT VICTIMS: PART ONE

Wed, 1 May 1963

Edinburgh Corporation: Letter from Children's Officer to Social Worker at Bangour Village Hospital about reducing maintenance payments for each child

```
EDINBURGH CORPORATION
   CHILDREN DEPARTMENT
      14 CASTLE TERRACE
           EDINBURGH 1
```

Dear Madam,

Mr. G. Millar.
6 East William Street, Edinburgh.

Further to your call at this department on the 30th of April regarding Mr. Millar's contributions towards the cost of maintenance of his children, at present in my care, I can confirm that I have decided to reduce the assessment to 15/- per week for each child. This decision has been made in view of Mr. Millar's present financial difficulties, as pointed out by you.

I shall still expect the outstanding balance to be cleared at the rate of 10/- per week, and thus a total payment of £2. 15/- per week will be required meantime.

I would like to take this opportunity of thanking you for your co-operation in this matter.

Yours faithfully,

█████████
Children's Officer.

GARY MILLAR

Thu, 2 May 1963

Social Worker: Letter in reply from Social Worker to Children's Officer about reducing maintenance payments

███████,
Children's Officer,
14, Castle Terrace,
Edinburgh, 1.

Dear Mr. Millar,

C/6988/9/7518/CMP.
Mr. Gordon Millar,
6, East William St., Edinburgh.

Thank you for your letter regarding Mr. Millar's contributions towards maintenance of his children. I am most grateful that you have agreed to reduce the contributions, and I'm sure Mr. Millar will be encouraged to continue paying the outstanding balance, as well as the current contributions each week.

This morning, I informed Mrs. Millar of your kind offer, and this has relieved her anxiety over the family's financial state considerably.

My thanks, too, to ████████, for his assistance in this matter.

Yours sincerely,

███████,
Social Worker.

SILENT VICTIMS: PART ONE

Sun, 5 May 1963

Bangour Village Hospital: Patient's Notes

```
5.5.63
```
Patient looking much brighter and happier.

```
11.5.63
```
Weekend Pass

```
12.5.63
```
Returned from pass.

GARY MILLAR

Sun, 12 May 1963

Dad: Handwritten request to Bangour Village Hospital requesting that Mum comes home for the Edinburgh May Holiday

6 East William St
Edinburgh 7

Dear Sir,

Mrs. Millar was so greatly cheered up at the weekend being home and able to visit the children that I was wondering if she could be allowed home again this coming weekend. As this will be the Edinburgh May holiday, I was hoping she could get home from the Friday until the Monday evening.

Yours sincerely,

Gordon Millar

SILENT VICTIMS: PART ONE

Mon, 13 May 1963

Social Worker: Report by Mum's first Social Worker

13.5.63

Interviewed Mrs. Millar on the ward. She told me about her weekend at home and said how she had enjoyed it. However, she said that she was worried about her home situation, and that bills, which she felt she could have coped with had she'd been permanently at home, had not been paid. She felt she would like to go home to keep an eye on her husband's behaviour. She had seen the children and was suitably impressed with their general health and progress. She spoke about Leslie's future, and still seems to feel that it would be best to have him cared for by an institution, though she is anxious that, should he become stronger and more capable, she should have free access to him and be free to take him home.

Home visit to Mr. Millar.

He was pleased with the way his wife had coped with her weekend and had enjoyed having her. A lot of money had been spent on taking her out for meals, and this had meant that he had not managed to get everything paid up. The Children's Department has been paid.

He was, I felt, unjustifiably optimistic about getting out of his financial tangle, but I felt that he was making quite a fair effort, considering his limitations.

Mon, 13 May 1963

Bangour Village Hospital: Letter from Physician Superintendent to Dad confirming request for Weekend Pass from 17.05.63 to 20.05.63

```
                            Mr. Gordon Millar,
                       6, East William Street,
                              EDINBURGH, 7.
```

Dear Sir,

Thank you for your letter concerning your wife. It will be in order for Mrs. Millar to go home this weekend from Friday 17th May until Monday evening 20th May, arriving back not later than 7 o'clock.

Yours faithfully,

██████████,
Physician Superintendent.

SILENT VICTIMS: PART ONE

Tue, 14 May 1963

Social Worker: Report by Mum's first Social Worker

14.5.63

Conversation with ▮▮▮▮▮▮▮▮, Almoner, Sick Children's Hospital. Asked her to find out for me what the views of Leslie's doctors were as to the best way of caring for him, and explained that it was felt by Mrs. Millar and the staff here that it might be best for the family if residential care was found for him. ▮▮▮▮▮▮▮ (Almoner) agreed to discuss this with the doctors, and to inform me of their opinions on the matter.

16.5.63

Visit to Family Planning Clinic, Dean Terrace. ▮▮▮▮▮▮▮ had given Mrs. Millar a letter explaining the very unfortunate side effects which her contraceptive pills were having. The doctors at the clinic felt that Mrs. Millar must be seen by a consultant gynaecologist at the Royal immediately. This was arranged and I accompanied her there.

Fri, 17 May 1963

Bangour Village Hospital: Patient's Notes

Weekend Pass until Tuesday, 21st.

21.5.63

Returned from pass.

GARY MILLAR

Tue, 21 May 1963

Dad: Handwritten request to Bangour Village Hospital requesting that Mum comes home for the next weekend. However, she was discharged on 22.05.63.

```
                                  6 East William St
                                       Edinburgh 7

   Dear Sir,

I thank you for granting Mrs. Margaret M. Millar
a weekend pass for the holiday weekend.
   I hereby request that Mrs. Millar be granted
leave again this coming week

   I remain
   Yours Sincerely

   Gordon Millar
```

SILENT VICTIMS: PART ONE

Wed, 22 May 1963

Bangour Village Hospital: Discharge (admission from 12.04.63 - 22.05.63)

22.5.63
```
Date of Discharge: 22.05.63
```

Wed, 22 May 1963

Social Worker: Report by Mum's first Social Worker

22.5.63
```
Interview in office. Mrs. Millar was very
worried about financial matters at home. The
Electricity Board have threatened to cut off the
electricity, and bills have not been paid. She
felt she could manage better herself than her
husband had been doing, although she showed no
anger at the way he had handled their affairs
and said that he had done his best.
  Mrs. Millar was home at the weekend and said
she enjoyed herself, and had been taken to
Whitley Bay by her father. She felt she could
cope at home if the children could stay in care
for two weeks after she went home, to give her
time to settle.
  Later, Mrs. Millar came to tell me she was
going home, and we arranged that I should visit
on Friday or Monday morning.
```

GARY MILLAR

Fri, 24 May 1963

Social Worker: Letter in reply from Social Worker to the Almoner, Sick Children's Hospital about keeping Leslie in their care

███████,
Almoner,
Royal Hospital for Sick Children,
Sciences Road,
Edinburgh, 9.

Dear ███████,

LESLIE MILLAR, 6, East William Street, Edinburgh. D.of B. 20.3.62.

Thank you for your very helpful letter about Leslie, and for the arrangements you have suggested for his care. I have discussed these with Mrs. Millar's doctor here, and she feels that they would be very suitable.

Mrs. Millar was discharged from here on Wednesday evening, mainly because of her extreme anxiety about home affairs. I will be visiting her on Monday morning. I will discuss your plan with her. I know she feels she would like to have the children at St. Helen's for about a fortnight, to give herself time to settle in at home. Would ███████ be able to take Leslie in again in about two weeks when the other two children go home? When I have seen Mrs. Millar, I will be able to give you a definite idea of when this will be.

I am most grateful for the help you have given

me in this matter, I will keep you informed of any further developments.

    Yours sincerely,

,
Social Worker.

Mum, Grandad Archie, and Gary on a trip to Whitley Bay

Norman and Gary – Whitley Bay

FORTEVIOT ROYAL HOSPITAL

GARY MILLAR

FORTEVIOT ROYAL HOSPITAL

Forteviot Royal Hospital for Sick Children was based in Edinburgh's Hope Terrace.

The hospital was originally in the Sciennes area of Edinburgh. It provided services related to child and adolescent mental health, nursing and midwifery, community child health, and other specialised care. The hospital cared for over 100,000 children and young people annually from Lothian and beyond.

Notable properties included 14 & 16 Hope Terrace (which housed the Child & Adolescent Mental Health Services department) and 10 Chalmers Crescent (which housed the Lothian College of Nursing and Midwifery and the Community Child Health Department).

In summary, the Forteviot Royal Hospital for Sick Children played a crucial role in caring for Leslie and for other children and young people in Edinburgh until its relocation to a new facility in Little France in 2021.

SILENT VICTIMS: PART ONE

Mon, 27 May 1963

Social Worker: Report by Mum's first Social Worker

27.5.63

Home visit. Mrs. Millar was looking even paler than usual and was very depressed. She was very near to tears throughout the interview, and said that she feels very unwell, but does not want to go back to hospital. She was very tired, as she had been up nearly all night helping at the birth of her neighbour's child. This child had been a girl which had made Mrs. Millar very anxious, as she says that she has always wanted a little girl. It also made her wonder whether she wouldn't like to have another baby in the hope that it might be a little girl, but then she had decided that she could not cope with another childbirth, or with the child when it arrived.

Author's Notes:

One detail in the above information becomes highly relevant years later, but for privacy reasons, it is not something I can explore in this book.

I told her about ▮▮▮▮▮▮▮▮'s suggestions for Leslie's care, and she was quite pleased about these. She thought, however, that he would not be kept long in Forteviot. I assured her that in his case there would be an exception made. I stressed that there would be no difficulty about her having him home if she felt really able to look after him.

GARY MILLAR

Mrs. Millar was worried because she feels she can't be bothered to do anything about the house. She is also alarmed because she feels she cannot be bothered with her husband anymore; this, she says, is unusual, because up till now she has wanted him more than he seemed to care about her. This feeling she blames on her pills.

I suggested that I should visit the next day, and she was keen that I should. She was obviously very alarmed by her inability to settle into her home situation, and I felt that her protestations that she did not want to come back to hospital were probably covering a wish to do so.

28.5.63

Mrs. Millar looks slightly better, but is still depressed, says she has no energy and does not want to bother to keep her house clean, and feels guilty that she has not done what she feels is very little for her neighbour who has just had the baby. I reassured her that she had done more than ever could have been expected of her in the circumstances.

Mrs. Millar mentioned the drugs she is on – Melleril and her contraceptive pills – and said she did not think the Melleril tablets were doing her any good, and that she thought the other ones were responsible for a lot of her troubles. She is still producing milk. From this, she went on to talk about being sterilised and expressed a wish to have an operation done, and to be finished with all the worries of contraception.

She said that even the thought of a little girl would not make her want to have another baby.

Mr. Millar came in, and once he had settled

SILENT VICTIMS: PART ONE

in, I asked him how he had found her. They were both amused by the fact that on one occasion when she had asked him to help her to clear out the house, she had left him to do all the work and had gone to visit a neighbour. He related the story at great length, and they both seemed to feel it was a good joke.

We talked about the children and Mr. Millar seemed to be more satisfied with the arrangements suggested for Leslie's care. Mrs. Millar brought up the question of her sterilisation. I stressed that this was a matter for both of them to decide and encouraged Mr. Millar to share his views on the subject. He said that he felt he had reached the stage now where he could see this from her point of view, but when he was younger, he would've said that she was there to have children and would not have considered the matter further. He felt it would be beneficial to her health to be sterilised - then he remembered what she has said when she has seen her neighbour's little girl.

Mrs. Millar was in tears when we talked about the children and said she wished she could cope, and that she felt she ought to be able to. She quoted examples of woman who had far more children than she had and seem to be able to cope with them. It was pointed out that they had their problems too. She seemed to be afraid all the time, and says frequently, that she hopes people would not shout at her or 'give her a row' - her GP, ███████, me, her husband. It was pointed out that none had yet shouted at her.

The conversation turned to their financial matters, about which they are both very unrealistic. The electricity has been paid, the children's bill is paid regularly, and Mrs.

Millar thinks she can pay everything else in turn. I suggested again that they work it out together on paper, saying how well Mr. Millar had written out a list of his commitments before for me. They told me what efforts they had made in the past, and they could try again.

We talked until Mrs. Millar was looking brighter, and I arranged that she would see me after she had seen ███████ tomorrow (29.5.63).

Author's Notes:
Combining Melleril (thioridazine) with contraceptive pills might lead to interactions and may affect the effectiveness of both medications.

SILENT VICTIMS: PART ONE

Mon, 3 June 1963

Social Worker: Report by Mum's first Social Worker. Hospitalised due to an overdose of unexplained drugs.

3.6.63

Mr. Millar phoned to tell me that on Friday night Mrs. Millar had taken an overdose of tablets (he thought 24) and had been unconscious until Sunday. She is now in the Royal Infirmary and was conscious when he saw her this morning. He is still off work with a badly cut finger but felt he could manage by himself at home. I said I would visit Mrs. Millar in the evening.

5 p.m.

Spoke to Ward Sister, Ward 3, R.I.E., who said that although Mrs. Millar was rather better now, she was feeling very sorry for herself and would do nothing to help herself. She had left a suicide note but does not appear to remember anything about what happened and says she does not know why she did it.

Mrs. Millar herself was very depressed and told me she could remember nothing about her attempt. She is stiff all over, because her husband and GP had slapped her repeatedly to try to bring her round. She kept wondering what ▆▆▆▆▆▆▆ would say and what various people's reactions to her attempt had been. She told me that her husband had phoned all their relatives and told them and seemed to resent this.

She was very miserable and looked very tired.

GARY MILLAR

5.6.63

Visit to Royal. Mrs. Millar saying she does not want to come back into hospital, although she hates East William Street. She was still very depressed and apathetic and looked very tired.

Her husband has been to see her, and they had quarrelled slightly. He has said that she preferred being in hospital to being at home, and she had told him not to come back, as he upset her.

Mrs. Millar said that everyone else was trying to push her back into hospital, and that she felt that entry into hospital was not voluntary in her case. I explained that no one could force her to go into hospital, and that she must make up her own mind, but she should take into consideration any medical advice given her.

SILENT VICTIMS: PART ONE

Wed, 5 June 1963

Bangour Village Hospital: Letter from Registrar to GP about Mum's attempted suicide on 31.05.63

▮▮▮▮▮▮,
16, Windsor Street,
EDINBURGH.

Dear ▮▮▮▮▮▮,

MARGARET MILLAR, 6 East William Street, Edinburgh.

This is the woman about whom I spoke to you the other day on the telephone, after I had seen her as an out-patient. She was re-admitted to us on 12.4.63 and discharged on 22.5.63. As you know, we said that the prognosis was very bad, and this has been quickly proved correct as you no doubt know she attempted suicide on Friday evening. I believe she will be returning to us from the Royal Infirmary as soon as we have a bed.

Yours sincerely.

▮▮▮▮▮▮,
Registrar.

GARY MILLAR

Thu, 13 June 1963

Social Worker: Letter from Social Worker to Mum about Leslie staying at St. Helen's and confirming their next appointment for 17.06.63.

```
                                    Mrs. Millar,
                          6, East William Street,
                                       EDINBURGH.
```

Dear Mrs. Millar,

I am afraid that I will not be able to visit you on Friday afternoon. I have, however, contacted the matron at St. Helen's, who is willing to keep Leslie just now, until the Sick Children's Hospital can take him. ▆▆▆▆▆▆▆, the Almoner there, is on holiday this week, but I will speak to her about Leslie when she returns. Matron agreed that it would be best if you saw only Gary and Norman when you go to the nursery in the afternoon.

I would like to come to see you and the children on MONDAY, 17th June, at 9.30 a.m.

With best wishes,

Yours sincerely,

▆▆▆▆▆▆▆▆▆,
Social Worker.

SILENT VICTIMS: PART ONE

Tue, 18 June 1963

Social Worker: Report by Mum's first Social Worker

18.6.63

Phone call from ███████████, Almoner, Sick Children's. Told her that the two elder Millar children were home, but that Leslie had been left at St. Helen's. She felt it would help the bed situation in Sick Children's if he were left there just now but says he can be admitted as soon as is necessary. She asked what we felt about Mrs. Millar visiting Leslie, and she agreed with me that she should be encouraged to do this.

20.6.63

Home visit. Both children and Mrs. Millar present. Mrs. Millar is still very subdued and rather 'faraway' looking. The children were cheerful, but Mrs. Millar says they are proving rather too much for her, and that she wishes she had come into hospital for a rest. She said, too, that during the day Norman is wetting and soiling. Neither child will go to the day nursery, and both are clinging to her. Later in the interview, at the mention of him going with his mother to visit other relatives, Gary (the elder child) became very tearful and said he did not want to visit.

I felt, from her remarks to the children, that Mrs. Millar was encouraging this attitude, though she says she finds tiring to be looking after them all day.

Bills are still coming in, and Mrs. Millar says this is worrying her. She still does not seem to have a clear idea of what her financial commitments actually are.

She told me about her last visit to the family planning clinic and said that the doctors had expected me to be with her. She was rather worried because she had been given different pills.

We spoke about Leslie, and I asked how she felt about visiting him. She says she will visit and would like to keep close contact with the Sick Children's, so that Leslie will not feel that his mother deserted him.

25.6.63

Home visit. Mrs. Millar was much more cheerful than she has been on other occasions. The children were lively, and Gary came to open the door by himself.

Mrs. Millar said that she was managing fairly well, and that she had been taken the children out as much as possible.

We spoke about her visit to the F.P. Clinic tomorrow, and I asked whether she would have preferred someone to go with her. She said she would, as she is still worried about the pills. I was unable to go, but explained that the clinic could get in touch with me at Bangour. We also arranged that she should come out to see ▮▮▮▮▮▮▮ in the afternoon and should come in to see me and tell me about her visit to the clinic. This seemed to satisfy her. She thinks the pills are making her tired, and she still has 'no time for' her husband.

We began to talk about her financial problems, and she made a few completely unrealistic suggestions as to how she could divide up her next week's income. We discussed the situation. Mrs. Millar told me what accounts she felt ought

SILENT VICTIMS: PART ONE

to have some payment made to them, and I drew up a list of these, and the amounts which I felt she might possibly manage to pay. She agreed to try to stick to this.

2.7.63

Home visit. Mrs. Millar had had her hair cut and permed and was looking cheerful and rather pleased with herself. She said she was feeling well and that she was managing the children. They were lively, but good humoured.

Mrs. Millar had been to see Leslie and was pleased with the progress he is making. He is to go into hospital on 3rd July, for a routine series of tests. She seemed quite happy about these.

She told me she had managed to pay something to all the accounts as we had arranged, managing to save £4 to the rent and £1 for her perm. Her husband's wage had been more than she had expected. I told her how well she had done. The whole family had been to the cinema on Saturday, too, and the children had enjoyed this.

Author's Notes:

The movie was most likely 'The Great Escape.'

Her husband came in and seemed in good spirits. He agreed that she had done well and said that things were being paid up quickly and was very noisy about how much he was giving her and what long hours he had worked to earn so much money. I noticed that Mrs. Millar became very much quieter and more withdrawn when he came in.

A neighbour came in soon after this, so I left, arranging to come next week.

GARY MILLAR

10.7.63
Home visit. Mrs. Millar was looking fairly bright. She was nursing her neighbours new baby girl, and obviously enjoying this, and kept making admiring remarks about the child.

The children were greatly excited by the fact that there was a mouse in the fireplace. Mrs. Millar said that her husband had caught four in the last half hour. She seemed to be taking this fairly calmly but said that the scratching of mice was annoying her very much at night. Mr. Millar came in, and when I asked if they had told the Sanitary Department, both expressed the opinion that nothing more could be done than they were doing. The whole building is mouse ridden.

Author's Notes:
This is one of my earliest memories. I remember being petrified by the sound of scratching under my bed. Grandad Archie thought he was being funny, telling me first that it was monsters under my bed, and later admitted it was mice.

Mrs. Millar had been asked to go to the Children's Department and had been told that the department could not take Leslie back. She had contacted Leslie's ward sister at the Sick Children's Hospital and Leslie is to be kept there until his transfer to Forteviot. She has been visiting him frequently and said she enjoyed doing this.

Both she and Mr. Millar were very optimistic about the way they are managing their finances. The rent is almost up-to-date, and other bills are getting smaller. The Children's Department account is almost clear.

SILENT VICTIMS: PART ONE

Mrs. Millar said that she and the children were all coming out to see ▮▮▮▮▮▮ (Author's Edit: The Registrar at Bangour Village Hospital) tomorrow, so I said I was seeing her then, and thus made my visit a short one.

Tue, 16 July 1963

Social Worker: Letter from Social Worker to Mum about confirming their next appointment on 17.07.63 at 4pm

```
                              Mrs. Margaret Millar,
                           6, East William Street,
                                         EDINBURGH.
```

Dear Mrs. Millar,

I am sorry that I was unable to visit you yesterday afternoon but will come today (Wednesday) the 17th, about 4 p.m., and hope this will be convenient.

Yours sincerely,

███████,
Social Worker.

SILENT VICTIMS: PART ONE

Wed, 17 July 1963

Social Worker: Report by Mum's first Social Worker

17.7.63

Home visit. Part of this interview was conducted on a bus, on which Mrs. Millar met me as she was going home from the Sick Children's Hospital, and as I was on my way to her house. She had been visiting Leslie and said that she had been quite happy with him today, but that on Monday she had been very upset, and her husband had said that if visiting him upset her as much as that she would have to stop going. When we had arrived at her house, she repeated this and enlarged upon it.

She said that her financial problems were growing less and seems to be pleased with the progress she is making. She was threatening, however, to buy new shoes and to take the children for holidays, which would mean that she would have to miss some payments. Tried to dissuade her from attempting too much expenditure.

Her own health has been fairly good, except that she has had a heavy cold, which has made her miserable. She has had few side-effects recently from her contraceptive pills; one breast has been sore and hard for a few days.

Gary and Norman are still clinging. Norman has not been wetting during the day. Gary has done once while in his parent's bed and while he was wide awake.

Mrs. Millar was complaining again about the mice which are over-running the whole building. Both Gary and Norman are apparently terrified of them, and so is she.

GARY MILLAR

Fri, 19 July 1963

Bangour Village Hospital: Letter from Social Worker to Mum about re-arranging an interview with the Registrar at Bangour Village Hospital and a visit from this Social Worker on Tuesday, 22.07.63

```
                                    Mrs. Millar,
                           6, East William Street,
                                       Edinburgh.
```

Dear Mrs. Millar,

███████████ will not be available to see you next Wednesday, unfortunately. I would like to visit you on Tuesday afternoon about 4.30 p.m. therefore, and we can perhaps arrange an interview with ███████████ later on.

With best wishes,

Yours sincerely,

███████████,
Social Worker.

SILENT VICTIMS: PART ONE

Tue, 23 July 1963

Social Worker: Report by Mum's first Social Worker

23.7.63

Home visit. Mrs. Millar has acquired a kitten, brought home from his work by her husband. She seems to enjoy looking after it and said that Mr. Millar had been very pleased at the way in which she had accepted it.

She seems to be coping with the children and the home quite well at present. They had been put to bed because they were tired this afternoon, but she said that she was managing them quite well.

She has had a real frank talk with ███████████, the Almoner at Sick Children's Hospital and said that this had helped her a lot. ███████████ had said that she could not tell Mrs. Millar that Leslie would develop normally, since no one really knew. She seems to have warned her that there is some fear of Leslie being mentally defective, and Mrs. Millar appears to be accepting this. She says that she told ███████████ that I had suggested that she might visit Leslie only once each week, if the visits were upsetting her, and ███████████ has said that this was a good idea, and was going to tell the ward sister that Mrs. Millar would be able to come only once a week.

Financial arrangements seem to be progressing fairly favourably, though Mrs. Millar is making rather wild plans for going on holiday in August. She has almost cleared a debt with one firm, and with the children's department, and has brought payments of rent almost up to date. She admitted, however, to having done impulsive buying of clothes; this was not so extensive as usual.

26.7.63
Interview in my office. Norman and Gary were with Mrs. Millar, and all three were in cheerful spirits. Mrs. Millar had had an interview with ▉▉▉▉▉▉ (Registrar) and was, as usual, enjoying her outing to the hospital. She still gives an impression of superficiality in her reactions. Arranged home visit for next week.

27.7.63
▉▉▉▉▉▉, Almoner, Sick Children's Hospital, 'phoned to tell me that ▉▉▉▉▉▉ wished to arrange a routine check for Leslie and was going to ask Matron at St. Helen's to send him to Sick Children's for about a week. It would be best if he could go back to St. Helen's after this, but as soon as necessary, he can be taken to Sick Children's on a long-term basis.

31.7.63
Mrs. Millar 'phoned to say that she could not keep her appointment here as the children were sick and had diarrhoea; ▉▉▉▉▉▉ (another Social Worker) took the call. Mrs. Millar said that she hadn't been keeping too well, had been 'awful tired' and wondered if it was the sun. She had said that she had been without her tablets as she hadn't managed to get to the doctors.

She asked that I go down to see her.

1.8.63
Home visit. Mrs. Millar was still rather

depressed and said that she had thought I would have come yesterday. She said that she is feeling very tired, and that the heat is bothering her. The children and neighbour's children have been quarrelling, the cat is a nuisance, and just everything is rather dreary.

I felt that this was temporary, as her main worries, which are her finances and Leslie, are no worse than usual. She says she has been worried about Leslie, and by her visits to him, and mentioned again the fact that she has now been told that there is a chance of his being mentally defective. She said that she could not have coped with him any longer. ▆▆▆▆▆▆▆ of Sick Children's has been talking to her about him and would like her to continue to visit about twice each week if she can.

13.8.63

Home visit. Met Mrs. Millar on the way there and she accompanied me back to the house. Mr. Millar was at home, taking the cooker to bits, so the atmosphere was rather unsettled.

Author's Notes:

Dad had a lifelong interest in fixing things and often hoarded items just in case they eventually became useful.

Mrs. Millar was complaining of tiredness and depression. She had sent the two children to bed for the day, as they had been naughty. They had been very mischievous in the mornings lately, but this is probably because she stays in her bed, and they are playing about by themselves.

Mrs. Millar said that none of her debts are being paid up while her husband is on holiday. She had borrowed money and bought two new dresses, as she is going out on Saturday nights now, with her father and a crowd of other people. Her husband goes out on a different night.

She then informed me she had been drunk on Tuesday night and had felt really awful the next day. Her husband chimed in cheerfully, that they had all been drunk and that Mrs. Millar had been doing the twist and everything. Mrs. Millar enquired anxiously of him if she had been crying for Leslie and was told that she had not. She said to me that she had been more careful when she was out on Saturday, as she was scared that she would start crying for Leslie when she was drunk and did not wish to do this in public. She said that she knew the doctor had told her not to drink.

When we were again walking up the street as Mrs. Millar was going on an errand, I warned her very firmly about drinking while she was taking so many tablets. She said she knew she shouldn't but did not seem worried in the least. She talked more freely about Leslie while her husband was not there. But both of them, while we were in the house, were showing less interest in him, she saying that he did not seem to belong to her, and he saying that everyone was alike to Leslie – a source of chocolate or other food. When we were by ourselves, Mrs. Millar talked of the expense she would have 'when Leslie comes out' saying that she would have to get him a completely new outfit of clothes. She is very possessive about his belongings and will not let any other children play with his toys, although he is unable to do so.

She talked about his ears, seeming annoyed that Gary has said that Leslie had no ears, and that she could not bear to think of people saying this throughout his life. She has never

SILENT VICTIMS: PART ONE

had him out without a hat on and is still wondering about the possibility of having ears grafted onto his head.

21.8.63

Home visit. Mrs. Millar looking tired, but not too depressed, although she was complaining of tiredness and sleepiness. She had not slept all night, and had this morning found one Sodium Amytal tablet in the cupboard, which she said she would take that night if she could not sleep. Her husband did not want her to do this.

The children were playing in the same room as we were talking, and were noisy, but seemed fairly settled.

Mrs. Millar was very thrilled to be able to tell me that when she had visited Leslie on Sunday, he had been able to move in his walking-chair, he had propelled himself along, by what sounded, from her description, to be a 'bunny jumps.' She says after this that no, she did not have room for him, as he would have to have a supportive walking-chair like this, and there was not room for one in the small living room.

She talked again about his hearing aid and said how she did not like it. She said that it made him look pathetic and that she would rather that they (the staff) tried to teach him without it. We discussed it and she said that she knew it was to help him, but she still did not like it.

She talked again of having another baby, saying that the only reason she wanted one was to have enough points to get a new house. And, of course, she added it might be a little girl. She said that her husband and her doctor did not want her to have one just yet, and that perhaps it wouldn't be fair anyway, as she had so much debt.

Last Saturday, when she was out, she drank advocaat and whisky, but said that she was alright. Her young cousin, who has left home and seems to be leaning on Mrs. Millar, had come in by this time, and said that it would be at the New Year time that Mrs. Millar would not be alright. Mrs. Millar agreed and said that she would miss Leslie and didn't want to make a fool of herself.

Told Mrs. Millar that I would visit twice more before I left, and explained, in answer to her question, how she could contact ███████ (the Registrar) or ███████ (other Social Worker).

Author's Notes:

This previous note clarifies that Mum's first (and main) Social Worker from Bangour Village Hospital for the past year was moving on, and they would appoint a replacement.

BEATEN BLACK
AND BLUE

BEATEN BLACK AND BLUE

This long-term Social Worker's last note is shocking. It highlights that Mum had lost her temper and had beaten me until I was 'black and blue.' Fortunately, I don't remember this occasion, but other similar situations I do.

I am now more surprised to learn that she had become desperate to have another child, this time a girl. I know she was still struggling with Leslie's difficult birth and his ongoing health issues. So, perhaps the comment about another house would have naively made some sense to her then confused mind.

Interestingly, three months later, I know both parents became incredibly supportive of Dad's sister Margaret, following the birth of her daughter Heather, the first girl born into our extended family.

SILENT VICTIMS: PART ONE

Social Worker: Final report by Mum's first key Social Worker

28.8.63

Home visit. Both Mr. & Mrs. Millar present. Mr. Millar did most of the talking and was very cheerful about his wife's health. She was quiet, and, I felt, a little depressed. She had lost her temper with the children last week, as they had been playing about in the kitchen before, she got up, and has spilt and spread about the house a mixture of soap powders, caustic soda, etc. She had beaten Gary until he was black and blue and had had to spend a considerable amount of time clearing up the mess which the children had made. Both she and her husband said that she was weepy for one day last week.

Mrs. Millar said how she wished she could have another child. She says that she wanted it only so that she could get another house, 'but, of course, it might be a girl.'

Her husband says that he was against her having another child at present, and so is the family GP. Mrs. Millar still clings to the mistaken belief that our doctor in Bangour tells her that it would be 'the best thing that could happen'.

Both parents had been to see Leslie on Sunday, and he had been walking very well with the aid of his walking frame. Mr. Millar said that if he came home, Mrs. Millar would have enough to do, looking after him.

SOCIAL WORKER CHANGEOVER

GARY MILLAR

CHANGE IN SOCIAL WORKER

Mum's long-term Social Worker's report, as shown on the previous page, is this individual's final known report? In fact, it appears that 55 reports have been written by this professional. They wrote their first note on 28.11.1962 and their last note on 28.08.1963.

There are no Social Worker reports after this point in Mum's case file covering her admission 'in a considerable state of agitation' to Ward 2, Bangour Village Hospital on 18th October 1963 and her discharge on 2nd December 1963. In addition, there are no referrals to the care system for Norman and me during these 45 days. Therefore, I am now assuming we were then being cared for by family.

A 27-week gap followed, before the next Social Worker began their reports. That new Social Worker wrote 11 reports - starting on 3rd March 1964.

Knowing Mum's constant need for help and the impact on her three boys, I do question what had happened during that 27-week gap?

Once I had sorted Mum's case file into chronological order, it was clear she faced significant personnel changes in those who previously cared for her. Her first Social Worker had left in August 1963, followed by Bangour's Registrar in early December

1963.

The next page shows the dates of all the first Social Worker's reports, and they are transcribed in full within the previous pages.

Nov 1962
28/11/1962

Dec 1962
04/12/1962
20/12/1962
31/12/1962

Mar 1963
07/03/1963
17/03/1963

Jan 1963
04/01/1963
14/01/1963
22/01/1963
23/01/1963
28/01/1963
30/01/1963

Feb 1963
05/02/1963
06/02/1963
14/02/1963
18/02/1963
18/02/1963
21/02/1963
26/02/1963
27/02/1963

Jun 1963
03/06/1963
05/06/1963
13/06/1963
18/06/1963
20/06/1963
25/06/1963

Apr 1963
01/04/1963
01/04/1963
03/04/1963
04/04/1963
26/04/1963
26/04/1963
29/04/1963
29/04/1963

May 1963
02/05/1963
13/05/1963
14/05/1963
16/05/1963
22/05/1963
24/05/1963
27/05/1963
28/05/1963

Jul 1963
02/07/1963
10/07/1963
16/07/1963
17/07/1963
19/07/1963
23/07/1963
26/07/1963
27/07/1963
31/07/1963

SILENT VICTIMS: PART ONE

Aug 1963
01/08/1963
13/08/1963
21/08/1963
28/08/1963

CONSIDERABLE AGITATION

GARY MILLAR

CONSIDERABLE AGITATION

The following notes confirm Mum appeared at Bangour Village Hospital on Thursday, 17th October 1963, in a considerable state of agitation. She said she felt she could not go on any longer. She accepted informal admission the next day.

The discharge date of 27th November or 2nd December 1963 remains unclear, as her notes include both dates. Perhaps the confusion is around whether she returned from her final weekend pass that began on 27th November and the official discharge date was still the 2nd.

The reason given for this admission, considerable (or acute) agitation is a state of psychomotor restlessness to overt aggression and violent behaviour. It can have various causes, such as alcohol or drug intoxication, psychiatric illness, or an underlying medical illness. Considerable agitation can also be an acute change in mental status with fluctuating symptoms.

Experts say that the 'Inadequate personality' described is characterised by persistent feelings of self-doubt, inferiority, and inadequacy. Individuals with this personality, like my mother, often struggle with low self-esteem, a lack of confidence in their abilities, and a pervasive sense of not being good enough. Those affected may have difficulty coping with criticism, avoid taking risks, and experience significant anxiety in social or performance situations.

GARY MILLAR

Fri, 18 October 1963

Bangour Village Hospital: Admission from 18.10.63 to 27.11.63

18.10.63
Date of Admission: 18.10.63

Inadequate personality.

Admitted from home Edinburgh at 12.15 PM.
  Pleasant and cooperative on admission. To have Amytal 25 mg B.D. and Equanil Tabs I B.D.
  Night report. Emotionally disturbed in PM. 3 Amytal gm III (ineligible handwriting) given at 10:30 PM.

18.10.63
9 stone 6 lbs

SILENT VICTIMS: PART ONE

Fri, 18 October 1963

Bangour Village Hospital (Ward 2): Admission Notes - includes possessions list, height, height, temperature, pulse and respn

```
18.10.63
IN POSSESSION ON ADMISSION

1 Pr Slippers
5 Cardigans
2 Jumpers
4 Nightdresses
1 Sanitary belt
1 Suspender belt
2 dresses
1 towel
1 coat
1 Wedding ring
1 Eternity ring
1 String of Pearls
Upper set of dentures
Purse containing £4-0-22
2 Brassieres
5 Pr Drawers
1 Petticoat
2 Pr Shoes
1 Pr Stockings

Height: 5ft 5"
Weight: 9st 8 1/2 lbs
Temp: 97
Pulse: 76
Respn: 20
```

GARY MILLAR

Author's notes:
Admission: 18.10.63 Discharge: 02.12.63 (following a week's pass).

19.10.63
Appears quite bright. Drugs administered B.D.

20.10.63
9 stone 6 1/2 lbs

21.10.63
Very pale, looking and listless. Blood spec to lab.

26.10.63
Appears a bit brighter.

SILENT VICTIMS: PART ONE

Sat, 26 October 1963

Dad: Handwritten request to Bangour Village Hospital to visit Mum on Thursday evenings and Sunday afternoons

```
                                    6 East William St
                                       Edinburgh 7
                                          Scotland
```

Dear Sir,

I am writing to enquire if it is possible to visit my wife, Mrs. Margaret M Millar on Thursday evenings and on Sunday afternoons, as I think that this will set her mind at ease getting news from home more often than at present.

Yours sincerely,
Gordon Millar.

Sun, 27 October 1963

Bangour Village Hospital: Patient's Notes

```
27.10.63
9 stone 7 1/2 lbs

29.10.63
Still    maintaining    improvement.    To    commence
Comorbid (handwriting unclear) E tabs nocte.
```

SILENT VICTIMS: PART ONE

Fri, 1 November 1963

Bangour Village Hospital: Letter from Physician Superintendent to Dad confirming visits requested on 26.10.63

```
                              1st Nov., 1963.
                           Mr. Gordon Millar,
                         6, East William St.,
                               EDINBURGH, 7.

   Dear Sir,

   Thank you for your letter. It will be in order
for you to visit your wife on Thursday evenings
and on Sundays. I am enclosing a Special
Visiting Permit which you should bring with you.

   Yours faithfully,
   ████████████,
   Physician Superintendent.
```

Sun, 3 November 1963

Bangour Village Hospital: Patient's Notes

3.11.63
Still appears to be showing improvement.

9 stone 7 1/2 lbs

6.11.63
Improvement maintained.

9.11.63
Condition unchanged.

10.11.63
Patient felt faint at 7 PM. Sent to bed. T.P.R. 97. 88. 20.

SILENT VICTIMS: PART ONE

Sun, 10 November 1963

Bangour Village Hospital: Patient's Notes

```
10.11.63
```
9 stone 5 lbs

```
11.11.63
```
Remain in bed today appears a little brighter this afternoon.

```
13.11.63
```
Blood spec sent to lab.

```
16.11.63
```
Overnight pass.

```
17.11.63
```
Returned from pass.

```
17.11.63
```
9 stone 4 1/2 lbs

Mon, 18 November 1963

Dad: Handwritten request to Bangour Village Hospital requesting a Weekend Pass for mum between 22.11.63 and 25.11.63

```
                                      6 East William St
                                          Edinburgh 7
                                             Scotland

  Dear Sir,

I am writing to ask permission for my wife Mrs.
Margaret M. Millar, Ward 2, to be allowed a
weekend pass.
  I shall be on a few days holiday, so that she
will not be alone at any time.
  If you could come home on Friday 22nd & return
to hospital on Monday 25th, I would be deeply
obliged.

  Yours sincerely,
  Gordon Millar
```

SILENT VICTIMS: PART ONE

Wed, 20 November 1963

Bangour Village Hospital: Letter from Physician Superintendent to Dad confirming request for Weekend Pass

```
                                 Mr. Gordon Millar,
                                 6, East William St.
                                    EDINBURGH, 7.

    Dear Sir,
Thank you for your letter. It will be in order
for you to have your wife home on pass over the
weekend. You may call for her on Friday 22nd
instant and please bring her back to hospital on
Monday evening 25th November, not later than 7
o'clock.

    Yours faithfully,
    ███████████,
    Physician Superintendent.
```

Thu, 21 November 1963

Bangour Village Hospital: Patient's Notes

```
21.11.63
```
Weepy and agitated this AM after receiving letter from husband. Seen by ▓▓▓▓▓▓ (Physician Superintendent). Reassured. More settled tonight.

Author's Notes: Was she unhappy about Dad's letter of 18.11.63 asking for a Weekend Pass? Did she not want to go home?

```
22.11.63
```
Weekend Pass till 27th.

```
24.11.63
```
9 stone 4 1/2 lbs

```
27.11.63
```
1 Weeks pass till 4.12.63.

Date of Discharge: 27.11.63

STERILISATION

STERILISATION

The following two pages include a suggestion by the outgoing Registrar at Bangour Village Hospital to Mum's GP to recommend her for sterilisation, highlighting that 'she is an inadequate individual, who is subject to bouts of depression and anxiety' and 'from time to time she is a considerable suicidal risk.' Clinicians believed that the procedure would decrease suicidal risk.

I am uncertain from the notes supplied whether her eventual sterilisation was entirely voluntary!

Eventually, the Royal Infirmary Hospital admitted her for sterilisation on 26th April, 1964. The operation took place the following day, and they discharged her on 7th May 1964.

Also, it would appear from this note that the Registrar was to leave the hospital within the week – assuming therefore that this would have occurred during the first week of December 1963.

I can only assume that this change in key personnel would have affected Mum's already fragile state of mind. It is obvious to me that, except for the Physician Superintendent at Bangour Village Hospital, professional commentary within her case file and medical and social care intervention appeared to reduce in the months that followed. This apparent reduction in support is against a background where I know Mum's mental and physical issues continued and became worse.

GARY MILLAR

Wed, 27 November 1963

Bangour Village Hospital: Letter from Registrar to GP about placing children in a home and the need for Mum's potential sterilisation

███████,
16, Windsor Street,
Edinburgh.

Dear ███████████,
Mrs. Margaret Millar, 6, East William Street, Edinburgh, 7.

This woman appeared at the hospital on 17.10.63, in a considerable state of agitation, saying she felt she could not go on any longer. She accepted informal admission the next day.

She has just been at home for a long pass (weekend), and I have seen her this afternoon before sending her on a week's pass prior, I hope, to her discharge. Nevertheless, as I said to you on the telephone, she may well require admission, in which case the children will have to be placed in a Home. As you know, she is a most inadequate individual, who is subject to bouts of depression and anxiety. From time to time, she is a considerable suicidal risk.

I think the time has come when we, perhaps, ought to recommend her for sterilisation. Certainly, there can be little doubt that she simply cannot cope with the three children she already has, and I think the fear of pregnancy is having a deleterious effect on her mental state. I do not think for a moment that sterilisation will solve all her personality problems, but it might, at least, decrease the suicidal risk. She has been having Melleril and I shall be grateful if you would continue to prescribe this for her. I shall be leaving the hospital within the next week, and ███████████ (Physician Superintendent) will be arranging for her follow-up if you think necessary.

    Yours sincerely,
    ███████████,
    Registrar.

GARY MILLAR

Thu, 5 December 1963

Bangour Village Hospital: Letter from Registrar to Edinburgh Corporation asking for further thought regarding housing change

```
                                    ███████████,
     Medical Officer for Mental Health Services,
                           Edinburgh Corporation,
                         Public Health Department,
                                  Johnston Terrace,
                                     Edinburgh, 1.

   Dear ███████████,
Mrs. Margaret Millar, 6 East William Street,
Edinburgh, 7.
   I wonder if anything more could be done about
this woman's housing problems. Her psychiatric
symptoms get progressively worse, and I think if
her housing conditions were changed, she would
be more able to manage her affairs and keep out
of hospital.

   Yours sincerely,
███████████,
   Registrar.
```

Author's Notes:
One of the last letters from the Registrar of Bangour Village Hospital before moving on.

SILENT VICTIMS: PART ONE

Thu, 5 December 1963

Bangour Village Hospital: Letter from Registrar to a surgeon at Edinburgh's Royal Infirmary Hospital about Mum's possible sterilisation

```
                              ████████████,
                                    Surgeon,
                             Royal infirmary,
                                   Edinburgh.
```

Dear ████████████,
Mrs. Margaret Millar, 6 East William Street, Edinburgh.
   I wonder if you remember this woman who was referred to you, so far as I can recall, from the Family Planning Centre, when troubled by her breasts. She was, at that time, taking one of the oral contraceptives, the name of which I cannot, at the moment, remember. You wrote to me at that time, but unfortunately, I cannot trace your letter. You mentioned the possibility of sterilisation, and we discussed it over the telephone, and I did not, at that stage, think it was a very good idea.
   Mrs. Millar has been back in the hospital between 17.10.63 and 2.12.63. She was in a very upset and depressed state, and, indeed, earlier this year she attempted suicide and was in the Royal Infirmary, Edinburgh, for some days. You may remember that there are three children of the marriage, and the youngest child has severe congenital deformities. It is since his birth that Mrs. Millar has been quite unable to cope with her everyday problems. She has always been a rather inadequate personality, but has been

```
very much worse since both of the last child.
   I would be grateful if you would see her
again, with you to assessing her as a
possibility of sterilisation.

   Yours sincerely,
   ███████████,
   Registrar.
```

Author's Notes:
Another of the last letters from the Registrar of Bangour Village Hospital before leaving their post.

SILENT VICTIMS: PART ONE

Wed, 11 December 1963

Royal Infirmary Hospital Edinburgh: Letter from Gynaecology Department confirming opinions about Mum's potential sterilisation

```
                                    WARD 36
                        THE ROYAL INFIRMARY
                               EDINBURGH 3

GYNAECOLOGICAL OUT-PATIENT DEPARTMENT


                              ███████████,
                       Bangour Village Hospital,
                        Broxburn, West Lothian.
```

Dear ███████████,
Re: Mrs. Margaret Millar, 6 E. William Street, Edinburgh.
Thank you for your letter about this patient, whom I saw again today. I can quite appreciate this patient is having extreme difficulty in managing the oral contraceptive, and I agree with you that sterilisation would probably be the correct approach. I understand that her own doctor also has this opinion, and that her husband supports it. I have therefore put her name on the waiting list and will get her into the ward as soon as possible.

Yours sincerely,
███████████

GARY MILLAR

Fri, 24 January 1964

Edinburgh Mother's Welfare Clinic: Letter to the Registrar at Bangour Village Hospital about Mum choosing not to receive contraceptive advice, by not attending an appointment

```
              EDINBURGH MOTHERS' WELFARE CLINIC
        (Branch of the Family Planning Association)
                                      18 DEAN TERRACE
                                   Telephone: DEA 1514

          ORAL CONTRACEPTIVE CLINIC


                             Bangour Village Hospital,
                                              Broxburn.
```

Dear ███████████,
Mrs. M. Millar, 6 East William Street, Edinburgh.

This patient attended our clinic here at the beginning of last year, but although she was given an appointment to return on the 15th of May, she failed to keep it and we have not seen her since. In view of her history, I thought you should know that she is not, at the moment, receiving any contraceptive advice from us. If you would like us to contact her, we should be glad to do so.

Yours sincerely
███████████

SILENT VICTIMS: PART ONE

Wed, 29 January 1964

Bangour Village Hospital: Reply to Edinburgh Mothers' Welfare Clinic by Physician Superintendent about Mum's failure to attend Contraceptive Clinic. Also confirming the Registrar was no longer on staff.

```
                              ███████████,
             Edinburgh Mothers' Welfare Clinic,
                          18, Dean Terrace,
                                 EDINBURGH.
Dear ███████████,
Mrs. M. Millar, 6, East William Street,
Edinburgh.
Thank you for your letter about Mrs. Millar
addressed to ███████████ (Former Registrar) who
is no longer on the staff here. It is good of
you to let us know that she has failed to keep
her appointment. I hope to be seeing her soon. I
will take the matter up with her.

Yours sincerely,
███████████,
Physician Superintendent.
```

GARY MILLAR

Sat, 8 February 1964

Bangour Village Hospital: Letter from Physician Superintendent to Mum confirming appointment at Sighthill Health Centre on 20.02.64

```
                               Mrs. M. Millar,
                        6, East William Street,
                                     EDINBURGH.
```

Dear Mrs. Millar,
I would like to see you again, and I would like you to come to the Sighthill Health Centre on Thursday 20th February at 5 p.m.

███████████,
Physician Superintendent.

MADE HOMELESS

GARY MILLAR

KICKED OUT BY DAD

Until I read this next note, I was unaware that Dad had ever made Mum temporarily homeless.

You will read in the pages that follow this day, on 29th February 1964, that she once again admitted herself to Ward 2 at Bangour Village Hospital after a brief stay at Edinburgh Royal Infirmary (there are no notes regarding her brief stay there).

She had also been seeking the help of the Samaritans organisation.

Against medical advice, she discharged herself one week later, on Saturday, 7th March 1964.

I also have no recollection that, during this episode, Dad's Mum had looked after us.

SILENT VICTIMS: PART ONE

Sat, 29 February 1964

GP: Letter to an unknown Doctor at Bangour Village Hospital requesting Mum's admission and that a psychiatrist sees her. Mum had been 'put out of her house' by Dad.

```
                          Mrs M. Millar age 30
                       6 East William St, Edin 7
```

Dear Doctor,
This lady is in an anxious depressed state and has been put out of her house by her husband. She has been admitted to Ward 3 on many occasions during the last 3 years and has also been an in-patient at Bangour several times.

She is now less agitated after nine grains Sodium Amobarbital orally. The problem now is her shelter and safety for the next 24 hours. She is temporarily homeless.

I should be obliged if you will admit her for 24 to 48 hours and have her seen by a psychiatrist.

Yours sincerely,
███████████

Sat, 29 February 1964

Bangour Village Hospital (Ward 2): Admission Notes - includes possessions list, height, height, temperature, pulse and respn and Treatment Card

```
29.2.64
IN POSSESSION ON ADMISSION

Coat 1
Purse 1 £6.6.10 1/2
Pr Shoes 1
Underskirt 1
Brassiere 1
Jumper 1
Cardigan 1
Skirt 1

Height: 5ft 5 1/2"
Weight: 9st 2 3/4 lbs
Temp: 97
Pulse: 80
Respn: 20

Treatment Card
3.3.64 Melleril 100mg T.I.D
3.3.64 Sodium Amytal gr 3 nocte
4.3.64 Ferrous Sulphate Tabs 1/1 T.I.D
4.3.64 Discharged against medical advice
```

Author's Notes:
Date of admission: 29.02.64. Date of discharge: 7.03.64 A.M.A. (against medical advice).

SILENT VICTIMS: PART ONE

Sat, 29 February 1964

Bangour Village Hospital: Patient's Notes

```
Date of admission: 29.2.64

                        Family doctor: ███████████
                           16 Windsor St., Edinburgh
```

29.2.64
Re-admitted from Edinburgh Royal infirmary at 3:30 am. Very sleepy and agitated on admission, saying her husband put her out of the house and she had nowhere to go. Seen by ███████████. Who ordered Sodium Amytal gr 3 at 3:45 AM. Same given and patient settled.

29.2.64
Rather emotional all day, wanting to go and see her children. She states she is not going back to her husband. She would take an overdose first. Seen by ███████████, who advised her to stay in hospital pro-tem. Also visited by husband this afternoon.

Sun, 1 March 1964

Bangour Village Hospital: Patient's Notes

```
Date of admission: 29.2.64
                        Family doctor: ███████████
                           16 Windsor St., Edinburgh
```

1.3.64
Remains irrational and agitated. Had hysterical outburst. Felt she must have some tablets. Settled without sedation and much brighter this evening.

SILENT VICTIMS: PART ONE

Sun, 1 March 1964

Bangour Village Hospital: Admission Notes for 01.03.64

```
1.3.64
Re-admitted after leaving her husband and
children after a row at home and seeking the
help of the Samaritans organisation.
   On admission, rather agitated and weeping.
Says she is worried about her children but
cannot face going home. States she doesn't get
on at all with her husband who has no interest
in her, is out all day and sits at home in the
evenings reading the newspapers.
   She wants to get away from her 'room and
kitchen' and would like very much the chance of
a new home.
   The children are looked after, two by her
husband's mother and the youngest physically
handicapped child has been admitted to the RHSC
```
(Author's Edit: Royal Hospital for Sick Children).
```
   Physically, Mrs. Millar looks pale, is rather
unkempt but is otherwise not incapacitated.
```

Mon, 2 March 1964

Bangour Village Hospital: Patient's Notes

```
Date of admission: 29.2.64

                    Family doctor: ███████
                    16 Windsor St., Edinburgh
```

2.3.64
Weepy most of the day and smoking incessantly. Complained of sore breasts and some bleeding (vaginal) probably due to discontinuing contraceptive tabs for another day. Husband visited this evening and patient demanded to be taken home and became very agitated. Seen by ███████. Given Melleril 100 mgs at 6pm with little effect. However, settled in later part of the evening.

Bangour Village Hospital: Updated Admission Notes for 02.03.64

2.3.64
Her husband visited the day after admission, and Mrs. Millar was only with difficulty persuaded from leaving with him.

SILENT VICTIMS: PART ONE

Tue, 3 March 1964

Bangour Village Hospital: Treatment Card

3.3.64
Melleril 100mg T.I.D

3.3.64
Sodium Amytal gr 3 nocte

Author's Notes:
Drugs Administered: Sodium Amytal. Gr 3 nocte instructs the individual to take 3 grains (approx. 195 milligrams) of Sodium Amytal at night. This medication was most likely prescribed for its sedative-hypnotic effects to aid with sleep (please consult the 'Glossary of Medical Terms' at the end of this book for further information about each).

Bangour Village Hospital: Patient's Notes

Date of admission: 29.2.64

Family doctor: ▮▮▮▮▮▮▮▮
16 Windsor St., Edinburgh

3.3.64
On the whole, the patient is much more settled and less weepy. Remains pale and a little tired looking.

NEW SOCIAL WORKER

NEW SOCIAL WORKER

Mum's newest Social Worker, who replaced her previous long-term Social Worker (whose own last note was dated 28th August 1963 – 27 weeks previously) wrote up this note dated 3rd March 1964, which is the first of 11.

This Social Worker's reports ended on 30th April 1965 (but there also appears to be a further gap of 47 weeks between that and the earlier penultimate report on 1st June 1964).

For me, these gaps are still a mystery whilst reflecting on what had happened during that first 27-week gap and the later 47 week one. This is further expanded upon in the case file note for Friday, 30 April 1965.

SILENT VICTIMS: PART ONE

Tue, 3 March 1964

Social Worker: Report

3.3.64

Patient seen on ward – looked ill and miserable. Said everything has suddenly become too much for her at home, the children, ill, and getting irritated by Leslie, slapping him. She had felt fine until the hospital made her have him home – she hadn't told ▬▬▬▬ (Author's Edit: Physician Superintendent) how she was really feeling. She had felt awful and had no one to talk to. I asked her if she had missed ▬▬▬▬ (Her former long term Social Worker) and she said it had helped a lot having her visit her, sorting things out together, the money, etc., but she realised ▬▬▬▬ (Her new Psychiatric Social Worker) on her own, couldn't come, she wouldn't have the time.

She said she was worried about things at home now and felt she must go out but felt she might just take some more tablets. I suggested I might call in the evening and see her husband – she seemed pleased and gave various instructions and messages.

Visited, but no one at home – visiting children at his mother's?

GARY MILLAR

Wed, 4 March 1964

Bangour Village Hospital: Treatment Card

4.3.64
Ferrous Sulphate Tabs 1/1 T.I.D

Bangour Village Hospital: Patient's Notes

Date of admission: 29.2.64

Family doctor: ▮▮▮▮
16 Windsor St., Edinburgh

4.3.64
Demanded again to be taken home by husband this evening. Seen by ▮▮▮▮ (Doctor) who persuaded her to stay and see ▮▮▮▮ (Physician Superintendent) in the morning.

SILENT VICTIMS: PART ONE

Wed, 4 March 1964

Social Worker: Report

4.3.64

Explained unsuccessful visit to patient ('patient's husband'). She thought perhaps he was visiting Leslie in hospital. Arranged to call tonight and she would let husband know when he visited this evening.

Later - again unsuccessful visit as husband remained at Bangour Village Hospital until 8 p.m. to see doctor.

5.3.64

Seen briefly on ward - she apologised for her husband missing visit last night. She complained of feeling confused and mixed up - not really knowing whether she hates the children or not. She thought she would probably go home on Saturday.

Housing problem, being reconsidered by Corporation any day now - but even if they get a house, she doubts if they would pay for it and she would need new furniture.

6.3.64

Rang ▇▇▇▇▇▇▇ (Medical Officer for Mental Health Services) re. housing - he feels very concerned about situation and will get in touch with ▇▇▇▇▇▇▇ (Doctor) straight away.

7.3.64

Discharged against medical advice

Sat, 7 March 1964

Bangour Village Hospital: Patient's Notes

```
Date of admission: 29.2.64
                    Family doctor: ███████████
                       16 Windsor St., Edinburgh
```
7.3.64
```
Patient   discharged   herself   against   medical
advice.
```

AGAINST MEDICAL ADVICE

GARY MILLAR

AGAINST MEDICAL ADVICE

Until receiving Mum's case file, I did not have any examples of her letters. Therefore, discovering this one is another emotional find. Albeit this one is much more distressing, since I know it has led to potentially significant consequences for her and our family.

As we know from earlier pages, when Mum was admitted to the hospital, she was rather agitated and weeping. She had said that she was worried about her children but could not face going home. She also says during this stay that she doesn't get on at all with her husband 'who has no interest in her, is out all day and sits at home in the evenings reading the newspapers.'

She stressed she wanted to get away from her 'room and kitchen' and would like the chance of a new home very much.

Yet, against this background, she still discharged herself and returned to a difficult relationship, to a home she hated and did so with ill health – both physically and emotionally.

SILENT VICTIMS: PART ONE

Sat, 7 March 1964

Mum: Handwritten letter to Bangour Village Hospital discharging herself against medical advice

```
I Margaret Marjorie Millar state I am leaving
the hospital against medical advice

Signed M Millar

Witness
```

FINANCIAL TROUBLES

FINANCIAL TROUBLES

You have previously learned that we faced financial difficulty throughout theses times, and I can confirm they continued well into the 1970s. We often lived hand to mouth, yet somehow both Mum and Dad found the cash to drink alcohol, chain smoke cigarettes, party, and dress well.

Therefore, I am grateful for the help from her two Social Workers and others. They tried their absolute best to help manage and resolve our growing financial problems.

The case file mentions interventions involving creditors – including care provision, clothing suppliers, utilities, rent, toys for Leslie, dresses for Mum to party on Wednesday's and Saturday's, and new slippers to wear whilst in hospital – ironically whilst complaining about money worries being a contributing factor to her emotional distress!

As we have seen, Dad had written out a comprehensive report about our family's financial commitments. He agreed the situation was grave and reported that most payments were in arrears. He sometimes blamed Mum for those difficulties, in return she blamed him. To help, he wrote to creditors to avoid court action, as he had received a warning about the expensive nature of court proceedings.

The successful efforts with the Children's Officer resulted in a reduction of payments for the official care of Norman and me. You will now read about other successful negotiations. Further suggestions to help reduce costs included sending back our rented TV set. Which we never did! They saw that as a drama too far.

Please note that where these notes say 10/- this means 10 shillings, or 50 pence post-decimalisation, or half of £1.

GARY MILLAR

Mon, 9 March 1964

Social Worker: Report

9.3.64
Visited – patient polishing the floor and asked me to excuse her if she just finished it and then she would make a cup of tea. The house was very clean and tidy, although she said she had slept till midday and only started to get cleared up this p.m.

She showed me a letter from Corporation saying no further priority over housing. She said this had upset her when she got it this morning, but seemed less despondent over it than might have been expected. We talked a little about finances and their commitments, but as her husband had taken the club books to pay them, we left it that I would call on Wednesday and we would discuss this further, and she suggested she should list her commitments. When I asked what sort of amounts were still outstanding, she said with some pride that she had always had big accounts with Ritchie's, £20 or £30 at a time – £10 was no use to her.

By this her neighbour had joined us, so I left, arranging to visit Wednesday late afternoon.

SILENT VICTIMS: PART ONE

Thu, 12 March 1964

Social Worker: Letter to Mum from Social Worker about helping reduce credit payments

Mrs. Millar,
6 East William Street,
Edinburgh.7

Dear Mrs. Millar,
I have had a word with the manager of R.G. Ritchie Ltd., and he has agreed to accept reduce repayments on your two books, providing that these continue regularly. We arranged that you would pay 10/- (instead of £1) on the one and £1 (instead of £2) on the other he has made a note of this arrangement.

I hope this will make things a little easier for you to get all the payments up to date.

I haven't yet had an opportunity of making an arrangement with Sloans but will let you know as soon as I can. I thought you might be pleased to know about Ritchie straight away and start the reduced payments on Saturday. The two payment books are enclosed.

I have let ████████ (Physician Superintendent) know that you would like an appointment to see you and he will be sending this to you.

Yours sincerely,

████████,
SOCIAL WORKER.

GARY MILLAR

Social Worker: Letter from Social Worker to Mum about revising the payments to Sloan's

Mrs. Millar,
6 East William Street,
EDINBURGH.

Dear Mrs. Millar,
When I rang Sloan's this morning, I learned that the supervisor himself is out on the district collecting and will be calling on you tomorrow. As he is the person with whom any different arrangement over payment will have to be made, it was suggested that you should ask him yourself when he calls. Perhaps you would ask him if he would accept 10/- a week instead of £1 for the next three months.

    I hope this can be arranged. I shall be interested to hear the outcome when I see you on Wednesday.

Yours sincerely,
███████,
Social Worker.

SILENT VICTIMS: PART ONE

Fri, 13 March 1964

Bangour Village Hospital: Letter from Registrar to GP about Mum's admission on 29.02.64 following an argument at home

▮▮▮▮▮▮,
16 Windsor Street,
EDINBURGH.

Dear ▮▮▮▮▮▮,

Mrs. Margaret Millar, 6 East William Street, Edinburgh.

This lady was admitted on 29.2.64 following a row at home and was in a distressed and anxious state on admission.

However, she settled well in the ward and her Melleril 50 mgm. t.i.d. was continued.

Her husband came to see her on Saturday, 7.3.64 and against medical advice, between them, they decided to go home.

Mrs. Millar's problems continue to be largely as a result of her inadequate personality and in the first few days of her stay, she threatened that when one got home, she would take an overdose of whatever tablets she had in the house. While this threat should, of course, be borne in mind in view of her past history, it was told that nothing would be gained by enforcing her stay in hospital. We have made an appointment for her to be followed up as an out-patient and by further visits from our P.S.W. ▮▮▮▮▮▮.

Yours sincerely
▮▮▮▮▮▮
Registrar

Thu, 23 April 1964

Social Worker: Letter to Mum from Social Worker arranging a home visit on 24.04.64

```
                                    Mrs. Millar,
                            6 East William Street,
                                  EDINBURGH, 7.

  Dear Mrs. Millar,
I should like to call and see you on Tuesday,
(tomorrow) evening instead of Wednesday this
week  about  5  p.m.  I  hope  this  will  be
convenient.

  Yours sincerely,
  ██████████,
  Social Worker.
```

SILENT VICTIMS: PART ONE

Sun, 26 April 1964

Royal Infirmary Hospital Edinburgh: Mum admitted for sterilisation.

26.4.64
Date of Admission: 26.04.64

27.4.64
Sterilisation operation

7.5.64
Discharged from Royal Infirmary following sterilisation

NEW HOME IN BURDIEHOUSE

GARY MILLAR

NEW HOME IN BURDIEHOUSE

They placed both Norman and me in foster care between 27th and 30th April 1964. We developed chickenpox.

This note is the first sign that our family had successfully moved to Burdiehouse, an area in the southeast of Edinburgh, near Gilmerton and Southhouse, and near the town of Loanhead and the historic village of Roslin. 37 Burdiehouse Terrace was a stark contrast to our earlier 'room and kitchen' and its outdoor toilet. Our new home, a post-World War II prefabricated or British Iron & Steel Federation (BISF) house, had 3 bedrooms, indoor bathroom, a kitchen, a living room, and front and rear gardens.

Within minutes from our door and garden, once I recovered from chickenpox, I could hop, skip, jump and run across Burdiehouse Road and visit local farms and explore their wide-open adventure playgrounds. I especially remember these farms smelled of crops and livestock. I loved the smell then and still do today. Some of those fields are now home to a housing estate, an electricity substation, and a large retail park. The wide meadow in front of our new home (leading up to Burdiehouse Road) was also an ideal spot for us to play football. Very few cars drove along Burdiehouse

Terrace, and a solid grey stone wall protected us from the other busy road opposite. In this meadow, we would often play 'tig' with our cousins and we chased each other, shouting 'yer het' as our fingers brushed across fast moving arms and shoulders.

Sadly, my playgrounds of adventure and warm summer months, of fields of bees, tall wheat, balls of swede and turnip, mooing cows and neighing donkeys, exist no more.

Mon, 11 May 1964

Social Worker: Report about new home and sterilisation

11.5.64

Throughout March and April, patient has been visited at least weekly. The family have been re-housed at 37 Burdiehouse Terrace, a very short distance from patient's mother-in-law. Patient's admission to our R.I.E. for sterilisation was delayed on account of bad cough and some doubt as to whether she was pregnant again. She was finally admitted on 26th April, for operation on 27th. Her second week in hospital was very disturbed when she learned that the two boys who were in care with a foster-mother, had developed chickenpox and had been sent home. She pressed for her discharge a little early, telling the doctor that she could have help at home and that she felt fine.

Author's Notes: This note says the Social Worker visited weekly in March and April, however, there are no documents in the case file for during the second 2 weeks of March and only 1 in April. For example:

Mar 1964	**Apr 1964**
03/03/1964 Notes	23/04/1964 Letter
04/03/1964 Notes	
05/03/1964 Notes	
06/03/1964 Notes	
09/03/1964 Notes	
12/03/1964 Letter	
12/03/1964 Letter	

SILENT VICTIMS: PART ONE

Mon, 1 June 1964

Social Worker: Letter from Social Worker confirming Mum's appointment at Sighthill Clinic, 4.06.64.

>Mrs. Margaret Millar,
>37 Burdiehouse Terrace,
>EDINBURGH.

Dear Mrs. Millar,

▆▆▆▆▆▆▆▆ (**Author's Edit:** Physician Superintendent) has made an appointment to see you at 3.30 p.m. on Thursday, 4th June at Sighthill Clinic. I hope very much you will be able to keep this appointment.

Yours sincerely,

▆▆▆▆▆▆▆▆,
Social Worker.

GARY MILLAR

Wed, 18 November 1964

Bangour Village Hospital: Letter to Mum from Physician Superintendent arranging an appointment at Sighthill Health Centre on 23.11.64.

```
                            Mrs. Margaret Millar,
                         37, Burdiehouse Terrace,
                                       EDINBURGH.

   Dear Mrs. Millar,
I could see you at the Clinic at the Sighthill
Health Centre on Monday 23rd November at 6 p.m.

   Yours sincerely

   ██████████,
   Physician Superintendent.
```

FINAL SOCIAL WORKER REPORT

FINAL SOCIAL WORKER REPORT

This report is the final (of 11) by Mum's second Social Worker. The dates of these reports are:

Mar 1964
03/03/1964
04/03/1964
05/03/1964
06/03/1964
09/03/1964
12/03/1964
12/03/1964

Apr 1964
23/04/1964

May 1964
11/05/1964

Jun 1964
01/06/1964

Apr 1965
30/04/1965

However, this Social Worker's reports had a 47-week gap between 1st June 1964 and this final report on 30th April 1965. The Social Worker says here that Mum had been visited on average once a week, yet there are no reports for most of these visits.

Also, although this Social Worker reports

previously in her note dated 11th May 1964 that they had visited Mum weekly in March and April 1964, there are no reports, notes, or letters in the second 2 weeks of March and only one report in April. Maybe they didn't produce any notes, but it appears strange that there are none!

GARY MILLAR

Fri, 30 April 1965

Social Worker: Summary Report

Mrs. Margaret Millar,
37 Burdiehouse Terrace,
Edinburgh.

April 1965

Mrs. Millar has been visited, on an average, once a week for the past 12 months. During this time, she has had to meet a number of crisis and problems – Leslie was discharged from hospital in the summer, to await re-admission for a somewhat experimental operation on his ear. This has been carried out, but with no improvement in his hearing. Mrs. Millar finds Leslie difficult to manage and feels she cannot spend time with him trying to make him lip-read as encouraged to do by ▇▇▇▇▇▇▇▇▇, from Donaldson school who visits occasionally. Mrs. Millar is anxious that Leslie should be admitted to Donaldson's soon but is told there is a waiting list.

Gary now attends school and appears to enjoy it, but at first there was frequently difficulty getting him there as Mrs. Millar finds it difficult to get up in time to get him off. Recently this has been solved by Mrs. Millar's father staying with them, at first because he was off sick and laterally because he was unemployed. Mrs. Millar has mixed feelings about his presence but gives a general impression that he doesn't pull his weight financially.

Mr. Millar has remained at the same building job throughout the year and has, at times, deputised for the foreman. He has, however, been off sick for odd weeks, either for his gastric trouble or bronchitis – recently off work for two weeks for the latter. Mrs. Millar complains of financial difficulty whenever he is ill, as although paid, it is only his basic wage, but she also finds illness in her husband, very difficult to tolerate.

Finances

On moving to the new house, Mrs. Millar was determined to spend the barest minimum on extra furniture in order not to get further involved with HP or club payments, already quite extensive. During the following months, various new articles made their appearance, and at times bursts of new clothes. Mrs. Millar is not very specific about payments involved, but on three occasions has taken a part-time job as she said she needed the money, altho' feeling unfit to work. She is currently working in the evenings at the Pied Piper, but complains it is too much for her and against ▮▮▮▮▮▮▮'s (**Author's Edit: Her GP's**) instructions. Her father started a job three weeks ago so she may well be able to give up again.

GARY MILLAR

Tue, 6 July 1965

GP: Letter to Physician Superintendent at Bangour Village Hospital asking that they see Mum. The letter also highlighted Norman taking Mum's drugs.

███████████,
Physician Superintendent,
Bangour Village Hospital,
Broxburn.

Dear ███████████,
Mrs. Margaret Millar, 37, Burdiehouse Terrace, Edinburgh, 9. sometime of 6 East William Street, Edinburgh, 7.

I would be grateful if you could arrange to see this lady again at Sighthill. She continued with her Tofranil and Largactil till mid-May and then felt so well that she decided to stop them. Unfortunately, about 10 days ago, one of the children managed to get hold of the residue, and consume them, with very nearly disastrous results. Since then, Mrs. Millar has not been quite so well, as she feels that her husband and neighbours blame her for this occurrence:- with considerable justification!

The eldest child is also behaving badly and has endeavoured to set fire to the contents of the house on more than one occasion. ███████████ of the Sick Children's Hospital is taking an interest in the family and is consulting the Child Guidance Department.

Yours sincerely
███████████.

Copy to ███████, Royal Hospital for Sick Children.

SILENT VICTIMS: PART ONE

Thu, 8 July 1965

Bangour Village Hospital: Letter from Physician Superintendent to GP in Liberton confirming an appointment will be arranged for Mum.

```
                                      ▇▇▇▇▇▇▇▇▇▇▇,
                              6, Frogston Road East,
                                       Edinburgh, 9.

   Dear ▇▇▇▇▇▇▇▇▇▇,
Mrs. Margaret Millar, 37, Burdiehouse Terrace,
Edinburgh, 9.
   Thank you for your note about Mrs. Millar. I
had been told by ▇▇▇▇▇▇▇▇, our P.S.W. that
Mrs. Millar was not so well again, and I will
certainly be glad to see her. I will send her an
appointment for next Thursday afternoon at
Sighthill.

   Yours sincerely,

   ▇▇▇▇▇▇▇▇,
   Physician Superintendent.
```

Thu, 8 July 1965

Bangour Village Hospital: Letter from Physician Superintendent to Mum confirming an appointment at the Sighthill Health Centre on 15.07.65.

```
                                    Mrs. Millar,
                         37, Burdiehouse Terrace,
                                   EDINBURGH, 9.

   Dear Mrs. Millar,
   █████████ (Author's edit. Family GP) has asked me
to see you again, and I could see you next
Thursday 15th July at 4:30 p.m. at the Sighthill
Health Centre.

   Yours sincerely,

   █████████,
   Physician Superintendent.
```

FINAL
CASE FILE NOTES

GARY MILLAR

FINAL CASE FILE NOTES

My mother's case file ends with her Psychiatric Social Worker's only comments across all 150 pages. They relate to two visits and one specific note about Norman taking an overdose of Mum's sleeping tablets and my alleged bad behaviour.

Interestingly, the professional opinion stated that both Norman and I seemed to be demanding attention that we were not receiving, but we were not considered abnormal or in need of treatment at that stage.

Donaldson's School for the Deaf, otherwise known as 'Donaldsons' was renowned for its education of children with hearing impairments. Since its establishment in 1851, this school for the deaf has earned a reputation as one of the most prestigious in the United Kingdom. Its founder, James Donaldson, was a successful business owner who became profoundly deaf later in his life. He created the institution to assist deaf children based on his own experience.

During the 1960s, during Leslie's time, the school continued its mission of providing education and support to deaf children. The specific details of the school during that decade are largely unknown because of limited information.

GARY MILLAR

Wed, 18 August 1965

Psychiatric Social Worker: Report

18.8.65

Mrs. Millar seen again. Says she is feeling very well. Off tablets. Likes her work - evening work in a canteen.

Looks much more cheerful. Still thin and very pale and complaining of indigestion. No breakfast apart from endless cups of tea. Stays in bed late mornings. Still toothless.

Doesn't come to Wilkie House now. Says this is because of the job, but she never liked it much unless there was a special occasion.

23.8.65

Called again to see if Norman has been accepted at school. (███████████, Sick Children's Hospital had previously spoken to ███████████, about this, but the final decision lays with the headmaster).

Mrs. Millar still in bed 10 AM, but her father eventually let me in and reported that Norman is at school - just as well as Mrs. Millar had got him keyed up to go, bought him a school uniform, etc.

Leslie also is to go to Donaldson's as a resident pupil.

Phoned R.H.S.C. (**Author's Edit:** Royal Hospital for Sick Children) to let ███████████ know this.

Mrs. Millar is said by her father to be very well.

Note: There was much upset in the Millar household in July. Norman, the four-year-old, took an overdose of Mrs. Millar's sleeping tablets and was quite ill. He was in RHSC for five days. No after effects.

Mrs. Millar has got rid of all her tablets.

Gary (6) is said to be beyond control. Is said to be wrecking everything in sight: and Mrs. Millar has found a bundle of burnt clothing in the house which Gary set a light.

Both have been seen by ▇▇▇▇▇▇▇▇, Department of Psychological Medicine, but he does not feel inclined to take them on as patients. They both seem to be demanding the attention they are not getting, but are not thought to be abnormal or in need of treatment at present.

- END OF CASE FILE -

CONCLUSION

There we have it! 150 pages of sometimes distressing items of detail. 202 facts that more accurately highlight key moments in the social history of health and social care treatment between the years 1962 and 1965.

Someone advised me that there are no further records relating to my mother - a revelation I have no reason to dispute. But I wonder what happened to the many other instances where she continued to be treated beyond 1965.

I am happy to confirm that she gained some peace and happiness in future years, and often did smile, always with her top dentures in, but never her bottom set. She loved her overseas trips with Leslie and enjoyed her visits to Liverpool, browsing St John's Market for bargains that neither she nor we needed. She would stay with us for a month and on her return to Edinburgh, she would leave behind tons of bargain basement towels and bedding.

But there were still times in her later years when she would call me late in the evening in floods of hysterical tears. During those occasions, at best, she would exclaim that nobody loved her, and, at worst, she would threaten to end her life. These actions would sometimes trigger my own sad memories. I am

# ACKNOWLEDGMENTS

Fourteen years ago, prompted by my godmother Auntie Ina to research my family tree, I thought about writing a series of books about my family history. Not that my 4,627 ancestors are in any way interesting, but the Queen of the Nile piqued my interest the most. However, what is personally more relevant is my growing understanding of those that have gone before us, those that battled discrimination, conflict, poverty, and demons. Through time, thousands of individuals' DNA, loves, lives, legacies, and souls have intrinsically shaped the person I am now. So, I must first begin by thanking those ancestors, and of course, my living relatives and their loved ones.

Like all ambitions, time marches on, and employment and other commitments somehow impede completing our plans. However, 3 years ago we lost Leslie, my youngest brother. It is easy to say that he died far too young, but he most certainly left us before his time. A death from complications following COVID-19, plus the increasing physical deterioration of his spine and muscles, contributed towards his demise. His death prompted me to post my two page 'Lament to Leslie' on social media. With over a million views and a host of messages of condolence commentators asked me to write about him and his impact on our lives. As a result, I also use this opportunity to thank all those that prompted me to write — albeit slowly. Therefore, three years ago, following social media encouragement, I began drafting that book. In fact, it has been close to finishing since the end of 2023. So where is it? Well, being a belt and braces type of person, in parallel I reached out to Lothian Health Services Archive and others requesting my mother's health data and also my own social care records. While waiting for that data and expecting they would not release it, I put the first book that I had instinctively written to be about all five members of our family on hold. Those being Leslie, Mum, Dad, my brother Norman, and me. As part of my process, once my final draft of book one was complete, I asked 'beta readers' to give their opinions. Their response was, 'it is a powerful and moving tale of triumph over adversity.' They added it is 'both cautionary and hopeful' and 'it's important it achieves its full potential and reaches a wide readership.' I thank those readers for their support and guidance.

So why is it still not published? Well, I made the right decision, as when I received the information I asked for, it alters key memories from when I was between three and six years old. As a result, I have been updating my first book, by also removing any repetition and rearranging its flow. I now intend to complete that earlier book in time for publication in 2025 as part 2 to this story.

In the meantime, I found inspiration to complete and publish this book based on Mum's experiences over 3 years of her life following Leslie's birth.

Thank you to my husband and soul-mate Steve for his 43 years of undying support, my family and friends for their love and encouragement, the team at Writing on the Wall for their expert guidance, the NHS, mental health professionals, Lothian Health Services Archive (LHSA), the Scottish Social Services Council (SSSC), social workers and carers everywhere, Auntie Ina, my brother Leslie, and finally the person this book is about – my wonderful Mum.

ABOUT THE AUTHOR

Gary Millar, former Lord Mayor of Liverpool and a passionate advocate for social causes, has dedicated his life to helping others and turning adversity into positive action. Born in Scotland and raised in challenging circumstances in Edinburgh, Gary faced early hardships, including family tragedy, a brother's disability, and his mother's illness. Despite a difficult start, which included a series of foster homes and struggles with education, he found strength in his entrepreneurial spirit.

Gary moved to Liverpool in the early 1980s, where he reinvented himself. A graduate of Liverpool Polytechnic, he became deeply involved in the city's business and political landscape, eventually serving as a local councillor from 2008 until his retirement from politics in 2021. As Lord Mayor of Liverpool from 2013 to 2014, Gary championed diversity and equality, raising significant funds for various charitable causes, including those supporting vulnerable children, the homeless, and cancer charities.

Beyond politics, Gary has co-owned a number of businesses and earned numerous accolades for his contributions to business and culture. His work extends to supporting the care-experienced, people with disabilities, and those in need, as he continues to fund projects and initiatives that make a lasting impact on Liverpool and beyond. Through his dedication, Gary has helped raise nearly a million pounds for charity and helped countless businesses thrive. He has recently been made an Honorary Alderman of Liverpool in recognition of his eminent public service.

Today, Gary remains committed to his mission of 'Paying It Forward' by volunteering and focusing on positive change. His journey reflects a life of resilience, compassion, and dedication to making the world a better place.

HEALTH STATISTICS

When Mum was admitted to both the Royal Infirmary Hospital in Edinburgh and Bangour Village Hospital between 11th August 1962 and 29th February 1964, the medical staff measured her height, weight, temperature, pulse rate, and respiration. She was during her time in hospital re-checked for some of those.

Date	Height	Weight	Temp	Pulse	Respn
11/08/62	5' 5"	8st 8lbs	-	-	-
12/04/63	5' 5"	10st 2½lbs	97	84	20
21/04/63	-	-	98	90	20
18/10/63	5' 5"	9st 8½lbs	97	76	20
20/10/63	-	9st 6½lbs	-	-	-
27/10/63	-	9st 7½lbs	-	-	-
03/11/63	-	9st 7½lbs	97	88	20
10/11/63	-	9st 5lbs	97	88	20
17/11/63	-	9st 4½lbs	-	-	-
27/11/63	-	9st 4½lbs	-	-	-
29/02/64	5' 5½"	9st 2¾lbs	97	80	20

SILENT VICTIMS: PART ONE

DRUGS PRESCRIBED

Through analysing all the case file notes for those 3 years, I have been able to show the drugs that were prescribed to her and when. Sodium Amytal and Melleril appear to be mentioned more than others, closely followed by Tofranil. You will find further details about each drug in the 'Glossary of Medical Terms' that follow.

Drugs	Jul 62	Aug 62	Nov 62	Apr 63	May 63	Aug 63	Oct 63	Nov 63	Feb 64	Mar 64	Jul 65
Cyclobarbitone	X										
Equanil							X				
Ferrous sulfate	X									X	
Largactil											X
Librium			X								
Melleril		X		X	X			X		X	
Moditen	X										
Sodium Amytal	X	X	X			X	X		X	X	
Tofranil		X						X			X
Tryptizol				X							

SILENT VICTIMS: PART ONE

GLOSSARY OF MEDICAL TERMS

As this is a work of non-fiction and as a result includes several clinical terms and names of prescription drugs, I have created this glossary for ease of reference.

Almoner
An almoner historically refers to a person, often associated with a religious or charitable institution, responsible for distributing alms or charitable help to the poor and needy. The role of an almoner has developed over time and can vary depending on the context, but traditionally, almoners played a crucial role in providing social welfare and support to individuals in need. **See notes:** 01/04/63, 04/04/63, 14/05/63, 24/05/63, 13/06/63, 18/06/63, 23/07/63 and 27/07/63.

B.D.
Stands for 'bis in die' in Latin, which translates to 'twice a day' in English. It shows the frequency of dosing. Therefore, patients should take the medication twice daily, typically with a specified interval between doses. **See notes:** 18/10/63 and 19/10/63.

Cyclobarbitone
A barbiturate with sedative and hypnotic effects,

primarily acting through modulation of the GABA_A receptor. It has significant therapeutic applications but also carries risks of dependence, abuse, and overdose. Common side effects may include drowsiness, dizziness, headache, and nausea. Like other barbiturates, it has the potential for dependence and abuse. **See note:** 26/07/62.

E.S.R.
Erythrocyte Sedimentation Rate, a test that measures how quickly red blood cells settle at the bottom of a tube over a certain period, usually one hour. The results are typically reported in millimetres per hour (mm/hr). **See note:** 25/09/62.

Equanil
Also known as Meprobamate, is a medication used for the short-term relief of anxiety and tension, as well as for the management of acute muscle spasm. It is important to use it cautiously and under medical supervision because of the risk of side effects, dependence, and interactions with other medications. **See note:** 18/10/63.

Ferrous Sulfate
Also spelled ferrous sulphate, is an iron supplement treat iron deficiency anaemia, which is characterised

by low levels of iron, leading to reduced haemoglobin and a diminished capacity of the blood to carry oxygen. It can also prevent iron deficiency in individuals at risk, such as pregnant women, young children, and individuals with certain chronic conditions. Common side effects include gastrointestinal issues such as constipation, diarrhoea, nausea, stomach cramps, and dark stools. Taking the supplement with food can help reduce gastrointestinal discomfort, although it may also decrease iron absorption. **See notes:** 26/07/62 and 04/03/64.

GP
General Practitioner or Family Doctor.

Gr 3 Nocte
Instructs the individual to take 3 grains (approximately 195 milligrams) at night. **See note:** 03/03/64.

Hb.
The oxygen saturation level of haemoglobin (Hb), which is often measured using a device called a pulse oximeter. **See note:** 25/09/62.

Hypochromic
A type of anaemia characterised by abnormally low

levels of haemoglobin in red blood cells, leading to a reduced ability of the blood to carry oxygen to tissues throughout the body. The term 'hypochromic' refers to the appearance of red blood cells under a microscope, where they appear paler than normal due to decreased haemoglobin content. The prognosis for hypochromic anaemia depends on the underlying cause, the severity of the anaemia, and the effectiveness of treatment. With proper management, healthcare professionals can successfully treat many cases of hypochromic anaemia, resulting in improved symptoms and overall health. However, untreated, or severe cases of hypochromic anaemia can lead to complications such as heart failure, organ damage, or even death. Therefore, prompt diagnosis and treatment are essential for optimal outcomes. **See note:** 26/04/63.

Largactil
A brand name for a medication called chlorpromazine. It belongs to a class of medications known as typical antipsychotics or first-generation antipsychotics. **See note:** 06/07/65.

Librium
Also called chlordiazepoxide, is a benzodiazepine medication primarily used to treat anxiety disorders

and alcohol withdrawal symptoms. It provides effective relief for symptoms of anxiety but should be used cautiously given the risk of side effects, dependency, and potential for misuse. **See note:** 21/11/62.

M.C.H.C.
Mean Corpuscular Haemoglobin Concentration, which is a measure of the average concentration of haemoglobin in a volume of packed red blood cells. It is typically reported as a percentage. **See note:** 25/09/62.

Melleril
Thioridazine was a commonly used antipsychotic medication known for its effectiveness in treating psychosis but has fallen out of favour because of its significant side effect profile, particularly its cardiac toxicity. Thioridazine works primarily by blocking dopamine receptors in the brain, particularly the D2 receptors. This action helps reduce the symptoms of psychosis, such as hallucinations and delusions, which are believed to be associated with overactive dopamine pathways. **See notes:** 22/08/62, 15/04/63, 23/04/63, 28/05/63, 27/11/63, 02/03/64, 03/03/64 and 13/03/64.

Menorrhagia
A medical term used to describe abnormally heavy or prolonged menstrual bleeding during menstruation. It is a common gynaecological condition that can significantly affect a woman's quality of life and may require medical intervention. **See note:** 26/04/63.

Moditen
Also known by its generic name fluphenazine, is an antipsychotic medication primarily used to treat symptoms of schizophrenia and other psychotic disorders. It belongs to the class of drugs known as typical antipsychotics or first-generation antipsychotics. Moditen works by blocking dopamine receptors in the brain. Dopamine is a neurotransmitter that plays a key role in mood, behaviour, and thinking. By inhibiting dopamine activity, Moditen helps reduce the symptoms of psychosis. **See note:** 26/07/62.

Nocte
Instructs the individual to take at night. **See notes:** 26/07/62, 11/08/62, 29/10/63 and 03/03/64.

P.C.V.
Packed Cell Volume, which is a measurement, used in medical tests to determine the proportion of total

blood volume that is occupied by red blood cells (erythrocytes). It is also known as haematocrit. **See note:** 25/09/62.

P.S.W.
Psychiatric Social Worker.

Phenobarbital
A medication used primarily as an anticonvulsant to treat epilepsy. It also can be used as a sedative-hypnotic agent, although its usage for this purpose has declined because of safety concerns and the availability of alternative medications. Medical supervision is necessary when using Phenobarbital because of the risk of side effects, dependence, and interactions with other medications. **See note:** 14/02/63.

Pulse (P)
Pulse rate refers to the number of times the heart beats per minute (bpm). A normal resting heart rate for adults is typically between 60 and 100 beats per minute.

Respiration / Respn
Respiration or 'Respn' rate refers to the number of breaths taken per minute. A normal respiration rate

for adults at rest is typically between 12 and 20 breaths per minute.

Sodium Amytal
The brand name for amobarbital, a barbiturate drug that acts as a central nervous system depressant. It is primarily used for its sedative and hypnotic properties, but it also has applications in other medical and psychiatric contexts. Amytal works by enhancing the activity of gamma-aminobutyric acid (GABA), a neurotransmitter that inhibits the activity of neurons in the brain. By increasing GABA's effects, Amytal depresses the central nervous system, leading to sedation, hypnosis, and anticonvulsant effects. The therapeutic dose of Amytal is close to its toxic dose, increasing the risk of overdose, which can be fatal. **See notes:** 26/07/62, 11/08/62, 22/08/62, 08/11/62, 21/08/63, 18/10/63, 29/02/64 and 03/03/64.

Tabs I B.D.
Stands for 'tablets one bis in die' in Latin, which translates to 'tablets one twice a day' in English. This prescription instruction shows that patients should take the medication once in the morning and once in the evening, typically with meals or as directed by a healthcare professional. **See notes:** 18/10/63 and 19/10/63.

Tabs 1/1 T.I.D.
Instructs the individual to take one tablet three times a day. **See note:** 04/03/64.

T.I.D.
Stands for 'ter in die' in Latin, which translates to 'three times a day' in English. **See notes:** 26/07/62, 22/08/63, 21/11/62, 13/04/63, 15/04/63, 23/04/63, 03/03/64, 04/03/63 and 13/04/64.

T.P.R.
Stands for Temperature, Pulse, and Respiration, which are vital signs routinely measured to assess a person's overall health status. **See note:** 21/04/63.

Temperature (T)
The temperature reading shows the person's body temperature. A normal body temperature typically falls within the range of 97°F to 99°F (or 36.1°C to 37.2°C).

Tofranil
Known generically as imipramine, is a tricyclic antidepressant (TCA) that is primarily used to treat depression. Doctors can also prescribe Tofranil for other conditions, such as anxiety disorders and chronic pain. Tofranil is sometimes used to treat

bedwetting (enuresis) in children. Tofranil works by inhibiting the reuptake of neurotransmitters norepinephrine and serotonin, which increases their levels in the brain and helps improve mood and emotional stability. **See notes:** 11/08/62, 22/08/62, 12/11/62, 19/11/62, 21/11/62 and 06/07/65.

Tryptizol
Also called amitriptyline, is a tricyclic antidepressant used primarily in the treatment of depression. It can also be effective in treating other conditions, such as chronic pain and migraine. However, cautious use and medical supervision are necessary when using it because of the risk of side effects and interactions with other medications. It's advisable to avoid drinking alcohol while taking Tryptizol or any other antidepressant medication. **See notes:** 13/04/63 and 15/04/63.

W.B.C.
White Blood Cell count, which is a measure of the total number of white blood cells (leukocytes) present in a microliter (µL) of blood. It's an essential component of the complete blood count (CBC) test. **See note:** 25/09/62.

Taken during one of Mum's last visits to Liverpool

AFTERWORD

Writing on the Wall (WoW) is an award-winning Liverpool-based community organisation, renowned for its celebration of writing in all its diverse forms. Hosting two dynamic festivals and a variety of year-round projects, WoW embraces literature, creative writing, journalism, poetry, songwriting and storytelling.

With a commitment to inclusivity, WoW collaborates with local, national, and international writers, providing invaluable opportunities for individuals to nurture their creativity and share their unique stories. Beyond its festivals and projects, WoW's creative writing initiatives serve as a catalyst for personal growth and community development, promoting health, wellbeing, and fostering connections across diverse communities.

Whether you're an experienced writer or embarking on your creative journey, WoW welcomes all who have a story to tell or a desire to explore the power of words.

Madeline Heneghan and Mike Morris
Co-Directors
www.writingonthewall.org.uk